GOD'S NEW COMMUNITY

Graham Beynon

GOD'S NEW COMMUNITY

New Testament patterns
for today's church

ivp

INTER-VARSITY PRESS
Norton Street, Nottingham NG7 3HR, England
Email: ivp@ivpbooks.com
Website: www.ivpbooks.com

© Graham Beynon 2005

First published 2005
Reprinted 2007, 2008
Reprinted in this format 2010

British Library Cataloguing in Publication Data
A catalogue record for this book is available from the British Library.

ISBN 978–1–84474–481–7

Set in Dante
Typeset in Great Britain by CRB Associates, Potterhanworth, Lincolnshire
Printed and bound in Great Britain by Ashford Colour Press, Gosport, Hampshire

Inter-Varsity Press publishes Christian books that are true to the Bible and that communicate the gospel, develop discipleship and strengthen the church for its mission in the world.

Inter-Varsity Press is closely linked with the Universities and Colleges Christian Fellowship, a student movement connecting Christian Unions in universities and colleges throughout Great Britain, and a member movement of the International Fellowship of Evangelical Students. Website: www.uccf.org.uk

Contents

Foreword

Underneath its glossy and confident surface, our society is fragmenting. The problem is growing; some people are becoming more isolated, and though they are warm and well fed, it's cold comfort to those who need love and understanding as well as a couple of square meals a day. Others are not exactly lonely, but keep to their own little cliques. Wherever you go, people form gangs; youths on street corners, old folks in day centres, yuppies in wine bars, ramblers on hilltops. We learn to live in our own little subculture; we live by its rules and think with its prejudices. Sometimes the cliques gang up on each other. Everyone is working to a different self-centred agenda; behind the scenes, society is disintegrating. Isn't it about time someone thought of a way of reintegrating people, before it's too late?

Wouldn't it be great if you could get people of widely different ages, attitudes and outlooks to meet and communicate and learn to love and value each other? How wonderful it would be if children could grow up in a large extended family that includes the rich as well as the financially excluded, black as well as white; a place where class distinction or racial prejudice simply don't matter? If such an energetic mixed community committed itself to serve those who do not yet belong, imagine the impact they would have!

Communities like this exist: they are called churches. Churches are a great idea, they are God's idea.

But the trouble is, the twenty-first-century mind is clogged with misinformation about the church. 'A church', a friend of mine once said, 'is a building with a fundraising thermometer outside, proof positive that they are only after your money.' Christians are often no better informed and so the church fails to be all that it could be – a community of people transformed by the gospel, whose purpose, no less, is to transform the rest of society by faithfully proclaiming that same gospel.

This book is important because the church today is failing to be all that it could be. There is an urgent need to get a thorough understanding of God's blueprint; the text of Scripture itself. This book is important because it takes you through the seminal passages of Scripture that should inform our vision for our churches and because it encourages us to develop a truly Christian mind on the subject of the church.

The·author is well qualified to be your guide. He knows his Bible better than almost anyone I know, and he belongs to a superb church where the things he teaches are believed and practised – I should know, I was once their pastor and they taught me more than I ever taught them. Graham Beynon's deep knowledge, passionate commitment and practical involvement have equipped him for the job; you won't get a better teacher than that! Study this book and use it to teach others – before it's too late!

Dave Burke
Pastor of Bethany City Church,
a new church plant in Sunderland

Preface

About five years ago I gave a series of sermons on the topic of 'church'. At the time I was working for a congregation that was in the process of becoming independent from the church that had planted it. This move towards independence was a great opportunity to go back to basics and think through what the church was and how we would set ourselves up as church. Those sermons were very formative for me as I discovered in a fresh way from Scripture God's plans for his church.

Since then I've spoken on the topic many times, not least at an annual weekend away for a group from St Helen's Bishopsgate, London. This has provided a wonderful opportunity to rethink and reshape much of the material. While its roots in those sermons five years ago are still recognizable, it has been transformed in the intervening years.

Many other people's ideas and contributions are reflected in these pages. I have read and learnt from other authors on the topic and, more importantly, I have had the benefit of discussing 'church' with many people in a variety of different situations. These conversations have both sharpened and greatly enriched my own thinking. You can be sure as a result that the best insights in this book are not my own. I am profoundly grateful to God for all those who have helped in this way.

Along with my wife Charis, I would like to dedicate this book to the congregation of Rock Baptist Church, Cambridge. That was where the original sermons were first preached and it was with those people that we first began to learn what it meant to live together as church.

Graham Beynon
Leicester 2005

1 : A breed apart

1 Peter 2:4–10

I would like to invite you to join my personal campaign. It is only a small venture and very limited in scope, but I think it is worth joining. My friends tell me I'm a bit sad about it, too focused on details, but I can't let it go. 'What is it?' you ask. It's a campaign for Christians to use the word 'church' properly. Let me explain.

I had been in my position as an associate minister for only a few weeks when it struck me that I'd heard the word 'church' used in about six different ways. Some people used it of the building where we met on Sundays; they said, 'Let's meet at the church.' Others meant the large meeting room in the front of that building; when standing in a back hall they said, 'Let's go through to the church.'

I had heard someone else ask about the Methodist church, meaning the Methodist denomination, while someone else talked of 'the church in this country', referring to all the denominations and independent churches together. Others spoke of seeing me at church, by which they meant the main Sunday meeting. And finally, one kind soul had said how good it was to have my family as part of the church!

Which one of these comes into your mind when someone mentions the word 'church'? I hope that the image that comes into your mind would not in the first instance be of buildings or institutions, or even activities or services, but of the faces of people. When the Bible talks about the church, it is only ever talking about people, and a particular sort of people at that.

There's a passage in Peter's first letter that helps us to understand a bit more about church, and my little campaign, and why it's so important. The passage shows who the church is in two ways: people who believe in Jesus and people who belong to God.

People who believe in Jesus

When I was a student one of the discussions we used to have was about whether a Christian had to go to church. The outcome of these discussions was always something like, 'You don't have to, but you'd want to; it would be good for you to grow as a Christian.' That reflects a very common approach to church today – it is there to help me grow as a Christian, and so it is important, but not vital. It is something I ought to opt into because it is supposed to be good for me – even if the reality sometimes seems a bit boring.

Peter paints a completely different picture in this passage. He says: 'As you come to him, the living Stone – rejected by men but chosen by God and precious to him – you also, like living stones, are being built into a spiritual house' (1 Peter 2:4–5). Let's begin by asking who is this living Stone Peter is talking about here? He is the one who is 'rejected by men but chosen by God'. That can mean only one person – Jesus. And when Peter says 'come to Jesus', he means '*trust* in Jesus'. Peter makes this clear in verse 6 where he backs up what he says by a quote from Isaiah about the chosen and precious cornerstone that God has placed in Zion. In fact, this passage sees Jesus as being the one who divides the world into two camps. In verses 7 and 8, we have on the one hand those who believe in Jesus and to whom he is precious, and on the other hand, those who don't believe and reject him.

Those who reject him are like builders who look at a stone and say, 'That one's no good, we won't have that one.' But in fact, that is the stone which God has made the most important one, the capstone (verse 7).

So Jesus separates people; or rather people are separated by their attitude to him. There are those who believe, who come to him in trust, and there are those who do not believe, who reject him and stumble over him because they disobey the message (verse 8).

But our focus here is on what happens to those who believe in him. Peter says that as we come to Jesus, God is putting on his builders' hat and starting construction. He says we 'are being built into a spiritual house'. Peter has in mind here the temple in the Old Testament. That was the physical building where God was said to live with his people. When you went to the temple you went to 'meet with God'. But now, Peter is saying, those who believe in Jesus are being built into a new structure that God is putting together where he lives with them. The difference is that this time the bricks in the walls are people, they are *living* stones.

Occasionally you hear people refer to a church building as 'God's house'. And even if people don't use that language, many still think of such buildings as special places. That kind of attitude shows we haven't really understood this passage. In the Old Testament, you could speak of the temple as 'God's house', but now you can point at a group of people who believe in Jesus and call them God's house. We see the same thing in Ephesians 2:22 which says that people who believe in Jesus are 'being built together to become a dwelling in which God lives by his Spirit'. God is in the building trade all right – but he's building a house for himself made up of people, not of bricks and mortar.

Peter then changes the metaphor from 'living stones' to 'priests': 'to be a holy priesthood offering spiritual sacrifices acceptable to God in Christ Jesus' (1 Peter 2:9). As you trust in Jesus, you become part of a temple, *and* you become a priest in the temple who offers spiritual sacrifices. Again he's looking back to the priests in the Old Testament, who worked in the temple offering animal sacrifices. And he's saying that those who come to Jesus become priests, who offer a new sort of sacrifice, a spiritual one.

The Old Testament mentions two sorts of sacrifice. First there were sacrifices for sin, where an animal was killed to take the punishment for something a person had done. That sort of sacrifice has been fulfilled in Jesus' death on the cross, so we don't offer those anymore. And secondly there were sacrifices of thanksgiving, which weren't because you had messed up, but because you wanted to show your gratitude to God and your love for him. And this is the kind of sacrifice we offer now, but we do it in the way we live our whole lives (see Romans 12:1–2 for more on that).

So these verses in 1 Peter give us a picture of the church. It's a new group that God is putting together, a new temple where God lives, a new priesthood who offer him new sacrifices. This is why Christians could forget about the temple in Jerusalem once Jesus had come, because all that the old temple symbolized is now going on in the church, among those who believe in Jesus.

This has some simple but profound implications:

Church = people who believe in Jesus

This is what defines the boundaries of the church. Jesus divides people into two camps, either you're in or you're out; and it's those who trust in Jesus who are in.

By comparison, some people think that coming to church services or church meetings is what makes you part of the church. Or it's being on a membership list, or being baptized. But none of those things can make you part of the church – only believing in Jesus can do that. So we need to distinguish between those who come to the meetings and the true church itself, which is only those who trust in Christ.

Not that we want to put people off coming! I would love it if more people who weren't believers came to our meetings regularly. And of course they should experience the love of the community of the church without having to 'sign up'. But God cements them into the wall of his house only as they come to believe in Jesus. We need to remember that ourselves and gently point it out to people who come.

People who believe in Jesus = church

If you believe in Jesus, you are part of the church. To put it another way, joining the church isn't another decision you make after becoming a Christian. Peter said 'as we come to' Jesus, 'we are being' built. Coming to Jesus means you are automatically included in this new spiritual house that God is building, you instantly become a priest in this new priesthood God is forming. If you believe in Jesus, you are part of the church.

Remember the discussion I mentioned earlier about whether a Christian had to go to a church? The usual answer was that it wasn't compulsory, but it would help you get on as a Christian. No-one said, 'If you believe in Jesus, you are part of the church already.' But that's the truth of the matter: if you believe in Jesus, you are a member of the church whether you like it or not. So how are you going to live out your membership? That's the real question, not, 'Do you want to join?'

No Christian can say, 'I've got my relationship with God, but that whole church thing, well, I'm not really part of that scene.' You *are* part of the scene. If you have faith in Jesus, you are bound together with everyone else who has faith. You are like bricks in the same wall.

Of course, we might not always feel like we fit in, it might be hard work sometimes, we might even feel that we would like to get away from the rest of the church. But despite all that, we are part of it. As we come to Jesus, God builds us together.

So the assumption of the New Testament is that all Christians are part of a church. The letters are written to churches. When the word 'you' is used in the Bible it is almost always 'you' in the plural, that is, the group that is the church. In our culture, which is increasingly individualistic, this is a crucial point: we cannot be individualistic Christians. In trusting Jesus I am connected with others who also believe in him. We'll come back to this in the next chapter and think about it some more there.

Church = people

This point may be obvious, but it's so important it needs to be underlined: the church is solely made up of people. That means that any organizational bits of it, any institutional structures and especially any physical components like buildings are not the church. They are only things that serve the church.

We've got a joke in our family about this. When my daughter Cara was about four, she was very good at spotting classic Anglican church buildings. You know the ones built a few hundred years ago with spires and all the rest. She would often say to me, 'Look, there's a church, Daddy.' I'd agree with her, and she was very pleased with her church-spotting abilities. But one day it finally occurred to me that I was teaching her something terrible. The next time she said 'Look Daddy, there's a church', I had to say, 'You know that's not actually a church Cara, that's only a building, where a church meets.' And now if you are ever in our car, you might hear Cara proudly announcing, 'Look Daddy, a church *building*.'

The fact is that the word translated 'church' in our Bibles had none of the associations that the word 'church' has today. It could be translated 'gathering' or 'meeting' or 'assembly'. It could be used of any gathering of people who met for a particular purpose. It had nothing to do with buildings, or institutions, or even the activities of that group of people, it just referred to them as a group gathered together. That's why in the New Testament there are many references like, 'the church of God in Corinth'. That is, 'God's gathering in Corinth', the gathering of God's people who live in that town. Over time, of course, the word started to get used only of Christian gatherings, and then of Christian institutions and buildings and so on.

Our family usually walks to our church meetings on a Sunday morning. As we rounded a corner, the church building came into sight, with people arriving at it, and one of my sons said, 'People are going into the church.' My wife wisely pointed out that actually, 'The church is going into a building'!

And so we return to my campaign to restore the proper use of the word 'church' to mean those who believe in Jesus. In one sense, of course, it doesn't matter how we use the word, as long as we know what we mean by it. The problem is I really don't think we help ourselves. We keep slipping into thinking of church as buildings, programmes, committees, synods and institutions, whereas we should think of those people we know who also trust in Christ. My campaign doesn't have a lot of supporters but I'd encourage you to think about joining.

So Peter describes the church as people who believe in Jesus. But he also tells us something else about this group of people that make up the church; they are people who belong to God.

People who belong to God

In verse 9 Peter uses a number of different ideas to describe this group who believe in Jesus. He says this group is:

- *chosen by God*: he's singled them out, chosen them to be his, to be distinct from the rest of the world;
- *a royal priesthood*: they have new a relationship with God where they have access to him, and offer him sacrifices;
- *a holy nation*: they have been set apart by God;
- *those who belong to him*, literally, they are 'for his possession': they are those he owns.

There are a number of different ideas in that list, but I think they all focus on belonging to God. What is going on is that God is calling people into a relationship with him; calling people to belong to him, and to be distinct from the rest of the world.

Some people at our church have recently adopted a child. What were they doing in that process? They were choosing someone they wanted to care for, to grow to know and love, and to be bound together with. Now that they have their lovely little girl, you watch them doing all those things. They chose to adopt a child to have a relationship with her. And that's what God is doing with the church – he chooses people for a relationship with him.

However, the church is different from adoption, in that God is more than a parent. He is also the king we are to live for. So when God chooses people, it is like parents choosing a child, but it is also like a king choosing his subjects. God wants people who belong to him, whom he can live with as their God and they his people. That is the basic idea of church. God's people living in a relationship with God.

This point raises an interesting question: when was the first church? Some people talk about the Day of Pentecost, when the Holy Spirit came, as the birthday of the church. In fact, in one church I was in we sang 'Happy Birthday' to the church on Pentecost Sunday (to most people's embarrassment, I have to say). It is certainly true that something very special happened at Pentecost that affects the church, but that is not when the first church was formed. The idea of church is people belonging to God, in a relationship with him. So the first church was actually back in the Garden of Eden. God created people who were to live with him as their God, people who belonged to him. So Eden is the first picture of 'church'. We could even say that God created the world and people in it so there could be 'church'!

Adam and Eve of course then turned their backs on God and rebelled against him, and they were sent out of the garden and out of God's presence. The relationship was broken, church was over. But God immediately put plans in place to regain that relationship. In fact, we can see all of God's plans of salvation as plans to recreate church.

In the Old Testament, we see that most clearly in the people of Israel. It all starts with God calling Abraham, and then acting to save his descendants, the nation of Israel, from slavery in Egypt. God calls them to belong to him. Actually the phrases we have looked at from 1 Peter 2:9–10, are from the Old Testament, describing Israel. For example, in Exodus 19:5–6 we read: 'you will be my treasured possession. Although the whole earth is mine, you will be for me a kingdom of priests and a holy nation.' And in Deuteronomy 7:6: 'you are a people holy to the LORD your God. The LORD your God has chosen you out of all the peoples on the face of the earth to be his people, his treasured possession.'

These things were originally true of the nation of Israel. They were the 'church'. But we know that Israel was only ever a picture of what God would achieve in Jesus. And that is why Peter uses all these Old Testament terms now to refer to Christians. What Israel symbolized is now fulfilled in the Christian church. No longer limited to one race in one geographical region of the world, it has become a multi-ethnic, international community. So the church began in Eden, it was then restored in Israel but now is those who believe in Jesus.

Ultimately, the church will find its fulfilment when Jesus comes again and recreates this world. When we look at descriptions of the new heavens and new earth in the book of Revelation we find they are given in terms of this relationship, for example, Revelation 21:3 says: 'Now the dwelling of God is with men, and he will live with them. They will be his people, and God himself will be with them and be their God.' So when we think of 'church', we're talking about a big part of God's plans; in fact, it's the centre-piece of God's plans. God's intention was always to have a relationship with the people he's made. That's what was lost when we rebelled against him; that's what he has made possible again through the death of Jesus. And now as we believe in Jesus, we become part of this people who belong to God, who enjoy a relationship with him.

I hope you can see that the church is a key part of history; God's acts of salvation are so that he has a people who belong to him. He saves people to create the church. That's how important it is.

And so what God is involved in at the moment is the business of calling people to belong to him, through Jesus. He is building his church. He is creating a new restored people out of this rebellious world. Calling them out of darkness into his wonderful light, calling them to receive his mercy (1 Peter 2:10). God is forming a new people who belong to him; he's doing it through Jesus, and one day it will all be fulfilled and perfected in heaven.

So what do we get up to in the mean time? We'll be looking at the purpose of the church in a later chapter, but Peter mentions a couple of things we should be doing. First, *God's people declare his praises*. He has made us his people for a reason, 'that you may *declare the praises* of him who called you out of darkness into his wonderful light' (1 Peter 2:9). The phrase in italics picks up on a passage in Isaiah, where God talks about 'the people I formed for myself, that they may proclaim my praise' (Isaiah 43:21). People were praising God for what he had done for them; for his wonderful acts in saving them and making them his people. And it's the same here in 1 Peter: God is the one who has called us out of darkness into his wonderful light. He's the one who has shown us mercy in Jesus. And so we are to declare how good he has been to us. We are to declare his mercy and his kindness. God wants this new people he has chosen to belong to him to be people who praise him for it. That's one of our purposes as church, to tell each other, and to tell the rest of the world about God's goodness in Jesus. Institutions don't do that; buildings don't do that; committees and synods don't do that; only people who have been saved and belong to God do that.

Secondly, as his people we are to *live his way*. In 1 Peter 2:11–12 Peter says: 'Dear friends, I urge you, as aliens and strangers in the world, to abstain from sinful desires, which war against your soul. Live such good lives among the pagans that, though they accuse you of doing wrong, they may see your good deeds and glorify God on the day he visits us.'

Being a people who belong to God isn't going to be easy. Even though we belong to him, we still live in a rebellious world. We are now a breed apart within that world; that's why Peter calls us aliens and strangers. There is a sense in which we don't belong here.

And this should be our attitude – that this world isn't quite home. That doesn't mean we can't enjoy all the good things in life here and now. We are to love God's good creation. But it does mean we know we are different, and our real home is heaven. So we don't live like the world lives; we live as God wants us to. And, as Peter writes in verse 11, that means there's going to be a fight – sinful desires will war against our souls. We are like God's outpost in enemy territory, and we are in the thick of the fight. Life as a person belonging to God means living to please him in a rebellious world. And so in every area of life we will feel that battle. We will know the temptation to lie, lust, envy, boast and all the rest. But Peter says, as people who belong to God, abstain from those desires, resist them, fight back.

In verse 12 Peter goes on to show how our lives should be so different from those around us that they can't help but admit it. They might accuse us of doing wrong, and in Peter's day that was happening all the time, but he says we should live such good lives that our accusers will be won over. So we need to ask ourselves whether our lives look any different from those of our neighbours and colleagues. Is our attitude to money, possessions, status, sex, or friendship, any different from theirs? Is our behaviour in the office or the home any different from theirs? I don't like asking that question because I know how similar I can look. But I know we are to be those who live God's way, because we belong to him.

So will you join my campaign to use the word 'church' as the Bible does? And much more importantly, to *think* about 'church' as the Bible does? It's the group of people who believe in Jesus; it's the group of people who belong to him. And so it is the centre-piece of God's plans for the world.

Study 1
1 Peter 2:4–12

1. How would you define 'church' in one sentence?

Verses 4–8
2. What is meant by coming to the 'living Stone' (verse 4)? How do verses 6–8 help explain what this involves?
3. What does verse 5 tell us happens when someone 'comes to Jesus'? What Old Testament background is being drawn on here?
4. If someone said, 'I believe in Jesus, but I don't belong to the church', what would you say to them from these verses?

Verses 9–10
5. In verses 9–10 Peter is applying terms that described Old Testament Israel (Exodus 19:3–6; Deuteronomy 7:6) to the church. In what ways is the church similar to and different from Old Testament Israel?
6. List the terms used to describe the church in verses 9–10. What difference does this description make to how you view your church?

Verses 11–12
7. According to verses 11–12, as part of God's people how should we think of ourselves in relation to the world around us?
8. What attitudes and actions does this imply?
9. What has encouraged you or struck you about the church? What difference will this make to your involvement in the church?

2 : We are family

Ephesians 2:11–22

'*I have a dream that one day this nation will rise up and live out the true meaning of its creed – that all men are created equal. I have a dream that one day on the red hills of Georgia the sons of former slaves and the sons of former slave owners will be able to sit down at a table of brotherhood ... I have a dream that my four children will one day live in a nation where they will not be judged by the color of their skin. I have a dream that one day the state of Alabama will be transformed into a situation where little black boys and black girls will be able to join hands with little white boys and white girls and walk together as brothers and sisters. I have a dream today.*' (Martin Luther King)

These stirring words were spoken by Martin Luther King in 1963. And yet, despite all sorts of progress towards racial equality, we have to admit that divides between people of different colour, or race, or background continue today. The rise of right-wing political groups both in the UK and across Europe is ample proof of that. Further evidence can be found in the tensions that rear up over asylum seekers, or the occasional bursts of violence between different cultural groups.

A few years ago there was an interesting story in the news. A man called David Irving was involved in a libel case. The press referred to him as the man who denied the Holocaust really happened, and they claimed he was pro-Hitler and anti-Semitic. Not surprisingly he was called a racist by the media. But when he was asked if he thought he was a racist, he replied in a very interesting way. He said: 'I think we're all racist. I think there's something built into our microchip which makes us dislike people from different cultures.' And then he clarified the word 'dislike' by saying we have an 'instinctive emotional aversion' to people who are different from us. It's a challenging thought, isn't it, that we have an instinctive aversion to people who are different from us in some way; that differences of background, class, race, culture and age create some kind of barrier between us.

To a certain extent we have to agree with him. Most of us find it easier to be with people who are like us, whether it is age, or taste, or background, or education, or race. In other words, we find it easier to segregate. Just watch what happens when a mixed group is together at some event – when new people enter the room, they head for those who look similar to them! We all do it. It's our instinctive reaction to a situation.

Martin Luther King's dream is always going to be hard to achieve. Overt acts of racism might be outlawed, but you can't legislate for the attitudes of people's hearts.

We are united in Christ

This subject is of great relevance to the church. Paul, in his letter to the Ephesians, describes the church as a group of people who are united in Christ. Paul is writing to a church with different groups in it: Jews and Gentiles. These were two groups who would feel an instinctive emotional aversion to each other; they would segregate instantly. But Paul thinks that in the church such groups are united. In fact, Paul has three different parties in mind in Ephesians 2:11–22. The first is the Gentiles (verses 11–12):

> Therefore, remember that formerly you who are Gentiles by birth and called 'uncircumcised' by those who call themselves 'the circumcision' (that done in the body by the hands of men) – remember that at that time you were separate from Christ, excluded from citizenship in Israel and foreigners to the covenants of the promise, without hope and without God in the world.

This group is called 'uncircumcised' by the second group, that is the Jews; they are those who call themselves *the circumcision* (verse 11). And much of the passage is concerned with the relationship between those two groups. But there is a third party, and that is God. Tied up in the relationship between Jews and Gentiles is their relationship to him.

Paul is concerned to show what these relationships used to look like, and how they change though Jesus Christ. Diagram 1 helps to explain how these relationships were before Jesus.

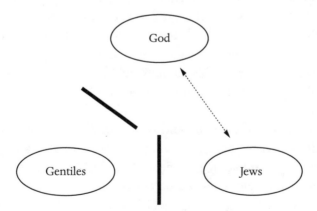

Diagram 1. Relationships before Christ

Jews and God

We mentioned in the last chapter that the Jews were God's chosen people in the Old Testament. Paul refers to this special relationship in verse 12 where he talks about 'citizenship in Israel'; that is, being a member of God's people. He also talks about the covenants of promise: the Jews had God's promises, that he would be their God and they would be his people.

In other words, there was a relationship between the Jews and God and that is why they are connected by an arrow in the diagram.

Gentiles and God

The whole point of verses 11–12 is that unlike the Jews, there isn't a relationship between the Gentiles and God. Paul is saying, 'You weren't part of God's chosen people, you had no part in those promises God made. In fact, you were without hope and without God in the world.' There was no relationship between the Gentiles and God and that is indicated in the diagram by the barrier that separates them.

Gentiles and Jews

As for how the situation used to be between the Gentiles and the Jews, Paul refers to the 'barrier, the dividing wall of hostility' (verse 14). Of all the social divides in Paul's day, none was wider than that between the Jews and Gentiles. The Jews referred to Gentiles as 'dogs' and considered them 'unclean'. And if a Jewish man married a Gentile, his family would hold a funeral for him. They thought that if someone married a Gentile, they were as good as dead!

That's hostility for you. And so in the diagram there is also a barrier between these two groups. There was also a physical barrier in the temple in Jerusalem. The Gentiles had their own court in that temple. They couldn't go beyond its confines because there was a barrier and a sign which said: 'Any Gentile crossing this line will be put to death.' So they were barred from entering, but the Jews could go further in, symbolizing the deep divide between them.

And that's how it was between these three groups. But Paul is at pains to explain how these relationships have changed in Christ (see diagram 2).

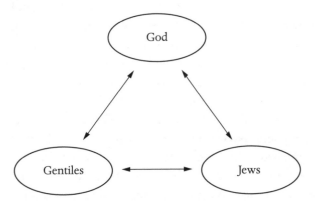

Diagram 2. Relationships after Christ

Gentiles and God

Verse 13 says, 'But now in Christ Jesus you who once were far away have been brought near through the blood of Christ.' We who were far away from God, who had no relationship with him, have been brought near to God by Jesus' death. Later, in verse 16, Paul talks about being reconciled to God through the cross, meaning being brought back to him. And in verse 17 Paul describes how Christ came to preach peace to those who are far away, namely, the Gentiles.

What all these verses have in common is that they describe how a relationship has been established between the Gentiles and God through the work of Jesus. Because of Jesus' death on the cross, we can be reconciled to God, we can be brought back into a relationship with him. Instead of being at war, we can be at peace with him. Verse 18 explains how we have access to God by the Spirit. That is, now we can have a relationship with God where we can approach him, talk to him, ask him for things, by his Spirit in us.

Jews and God

We've already seen that the Jews had an established relationship with God, but all that now changes in Christ. Verse 16 refers to Jesus reconciling both Jew and Gentile to God through the cross. And then, verse 17 says Jesus preaches peace to those who were far away – the Gentiles – and those who were near – the Jews. In other words, although the Jews had a relationship in the past, there is a work of reconciling and of making peace that still has to be done.

The difference it makes for the Jew is seen best in verse 18: both Jew and Gentile now have access to the Father by the Spirit. Previously a Jew's relationship with God was always through someone else. For example, the priests offered sacrifices for them, or the prophets spoke from God to them. Their relationship was always mediated through someone else – a bit like having to communicate through a third party because you can't speak directly to a person. But now, through Jesus, they can each have access to God as individuals. They have the Spirit in them, rather than the Spirit being only on a few. It's as if they have taken a step closer to God.

So what does all of this mean for the relationship between Jew and Gentile?

Jews and Gentiles

'For he himself is our peace, who has made the two one and has destroyed the barrier, the dividing wall of hostility, by abolishing in his flesh the law with its commandments and regulations. His purpose was to create in himself one new man out of the two, thus making peace' (Ephesians 2:14–15).

Jesus hasn't just brought peace between Gentiles and God and Jews and God, he has also brought peace between Jews and Gentiles. He has taken these two warring factions and reconciled them; he has made these two opposing groups 'one'. He has destroyed the barriers between them and united them.

When we think of Jesus' work on the cross we usually think of his purpose as being to reconcile us to God; and rightly so. But along with that he has another purpose. Verse 15 states it very strongly: 'his purpose was to create in himself one new man out of two'. Jesus forges them together into a brand new humanity.

And so, in the diagram we need to have a line between the Jews and Gentiles. Instead of a barrier and hostility, there is now a relationship. But, if you think about what Paul is actually saying, that change to the diagram isn't enough; it doesn't represent what is described here. The two have become one; the two have been made into one new man, so we have to put these two groups together into one new one (see diagram 3).

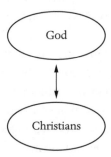

Diagram 3. True relationships after Christ

There aren't Jews and Gentiles in this new group anymore; we've got to replace those terms with a new category, *Christians*. We have Jewish Christians and Gentile Christians but they are Christians first and foremost. What they have in common in Christ is more important than whatever differences might once have separated them.

That is why this section is entitled, 'We are united in Christ'. Jews and Gentiles once were separated and hostile to each other, but Jesus' work on the cross reconciles them to God and to each other. Jesus creates a new humanity. One new man out of the two. And if that's the case between Jew and Gentile, how much more is it the case between us Gentiles. If this work dissolves that hostility, it dissolves every hostility; it breaks down every barrier between people.

You don't need to be a big fan of rugby to know that countries like England, Scotland, Wales and Ireland usually play against each other. If you watch any of their games, you'll see they play in fierce competition – especially when playing against England! But once in a while the British Lions are formed. This team is made up of players from all those countries. When they play for the Lions it is as if they take off their national colours, and they put on the British Lions colours. They become part of the same side, part of the same team. They now have the same identity and are united together, rather than being opposed to each other. So in Christ, it is as if we all take off the particular shirt that defines us, and put on the same shirt to become part of the same team, united together.

In the church it's not just the case that because we have been forgiven we ought to be nice to each other. It's not just that when we meet another Christian we both know God so we ought to be friendly. Rather, all of us who are Christians have been united in one new person, we have been fused together. And so we're now profoundly bound together in Christ.

The formation of a new family

To put this a different way, in Jesus there is the formation of a new family (verse 19): 'Consequently, you are no longer foreigners and aliens, but fellow-citizens with God's people and members of God's household ...' We are no longer a bunch of individuals separated by all our differences; we are united as God's people. We become fellow members of God's household. Jesus hasn't created a new club, or institution – he's formed a new family, God's household; that means we should think of ourselves as brothers and sisters.

Paul changes the metaphor in verses 20–21, but the point is the same: '... built on the foundation of the apostles and prophets, with Christ Jesus himself as the chief cornerstone. In him the whole building is joined together and rises to become a holy temple in the Lord. And in him you too are being built together to become a dwelling in which God lives by his Spirit.'

As we saw in chapter 1, God is building a new temple where he lives with people. But it's not a building of bricks and mortar, it's made up of people. And in this new structure God hasn't put together a bunch of individuals who belong to him but are unconnected to each other; we are bound together like bricks in the same wall. We are united in Christ.

This work of Jesus on the cross fits with what we know of our rebellion, doesn't it? When Adam and Eve rebelled against God our relationship with God was broken and we need to be reconciled to him. But their rebellion also broke our relationship with each other. It is because of that broken relationship that we have mistrust, hate, jealousy, anger, and all the other attitudes that destroy our relationships. It is significant that in the next chapter after the fall, there is the first murder. That instinctive emotional aversion we so often feel towards people different from us is a result of the fall; it's not how God made us.

But God's plans of salvation not only restore our relationship with him, they also restore our relationship with each other. So when we look at descriptions of heaven, what do we see but people from every tribe, tongue and nation united in praise of God. What a wonderful picture of God's new family perfectly united, with all barriers between them broken down. But in the meantime, that unity is to be seen in the church. John in his Gospel records the words of Jesus' prayer for believers. The last thing he prays for those who will come to believe in him is this: 'I pray ... that all of them may be one ... May they be brought to complete unity' (John 17:20–21, 23). Why? He goes on, ' ... to let the world know that you sent me.' Our unity, our living out what Jesus has brought, speaks volumes to the world about who Jesus is and what he has done. When a group of disparate people, who ordinarily would have no interest in each other or might even be hostile to each other, are united together Jesus says that helps the world see who he is and what he has done. That is how important this unity is.

Implications

The implications of this truth are far reaching. For example, it has implications for how we organize ourselves as churches. Once I attended a conference on student work in churches and the different ways that can be organized. One of the models on the table was of a church comprised only of students. And I was to preach on this passage in Ephesians the following weekend! I thought of what this passage says and I had to say at that conference that the idea of a student church was a terrible one. To have such a narrowly defined church doesn't tell the world very much about the unity Jesus has brought.

Ideally we want to see a multi-age, multi-class, multi-racial, multi-background type church. The more differences that are represented, the more the unity of the gospel shines out. Of course, a church can do no more than reflect the neighbourhood it's located in; there may well be a degree of similarity among its members because of that. If we start a church in a middle-class suburb, or on a council estate, people will tend to be from that area. So we can't contrive to have every difference represented, nor should we try to. But the point is, we don't organize ourselves to limit the breadth of the church.

Equally, once we have a church with lots of different people in it, we then need to be careful not to organize our activities in such a way that we segregate under one roof. We could have early an service that's designed for families, a later service for over 60s, an evening service for singles and students. And we have to admit that is appealing. That way we would meet people relatively similar to us; we would have a style of service we liked, we would sing only the songs or hymns we prefer. But that would be a denial of the unity Jesus has brought. As Paul says in Galatians

3:28: 'There is neither Jew nor Greek, slave nor free, male nor female, for you are all one in Christ Jesus.' And so I presume he wouldn't have been best pleased to see a church with a Jewish service, a Greek service, a service for slaves, and so on.

This is not to deny the value of specific groups in a church. At the church I'm at, we have a 'Senior Fellowship' for retired people, a women's mid-morning Bible study, men's breakfasts and so on. That's fine, so long as we don't just meet in our specific groups.

Perhaps the greatest area of debate here is in small groups – home groups or cells. It is easy enough in the main meeting on a Sunday to avoid people different from us. But it's not so easy when they are sitting opposite us in a small group! Any leader of a small group will tell you that makes for hard work. The greater the mix of people the more we have to work at our unity. We may be frustrated by other people in our groups because they are so different from us. It would be easier to have streamed groups of similar people. But if we are willing to work at it, the result will be groups of much greater richness, and groups where our unity in Christ actually means something.

All these issues have implications for how we go about organizing ourselves as churches. But perhaps the most challenging implications are in the area of our attitude. Some years ago I had the task of writing a constitution for a church. To give me some idea how to go about it, I spent time reading other people's constitutions. One of them had a set of promises that people who wanted to be part of the church agreed to. It included the following: 'We have a determination to welcome people different from ourselves for the sake of Christ.' People in that church made a deliberate decision to focus on their new identity in Christ and so to welcome people no matter what their differences.

That is exactly the attitude that is commanded of us because of this unity in Christ. I list some verses below that all say something about our attitude to each other, and they all of them stem from the fact that we are family in Christ.

- 'Be devoted to one another in brotherly love' (Romans 12:10);
- 'Live in harmony with one another' (Romans 12:16);
- 'Accept one another, then, just as Christ accepted you' (Romans 15:7);
- '... be patient, bearing with one another in love' (Ephesians 4:2);
- 'Bear with each other' (Colossians 3:13).

You see how important our attitude to each other is? And so we need to make a commitment to be devoted to each other, no matter how different we are; to live in harmony with each other, no matter how annoying we find someone; to accept everyone even when our instinct would be to reject them; to bear patiently with people even when they frustrate us. These aren't easy things to commit yourself to. They go against the grain of our nature. But this is how we are to live, because Jesus has made us a new family.

People of all sorts will walk into your church. They may come and sit next to you. They may be very different from you and you may be aware of the barriers that exist between you. Each time that happens, we have a decision to make: are we going to be pleasant and polite for a minute, and then excuse ourselves, or are we going to welcome them as brothers or sisters in Christ? And not just in that moment after the service, but when we see them week after week or when they turn up at our small groups.

But it's not just our attitude to new people we need to examine. You know how it is in churches, you get to know a certain group. Maybe you even sit in the same place each week. If you belong to a large church, there may be loads of people you recognize but who you don't know and never talk to. Some of that is inevitable, but as much as anything it is our attitude that keeps us within the group we know and like.

We need a radical change of attitude. We need to regard everyone in the church as a brother and a sister. And so our attitude should be one of care and concern, one of warmth and love, because Jesus has united us as a family and these are the attributes God wants to see in his family.

So when you arrive at your church on a Sunday, or you walk into your small group midweek, why not look around at the people there and say to yourself, 'Family – this is my family.' Whether you know them very well, whether you like them very much, tell yourself, 'These are my brothers and sisters; I'm united with this group.'

Martin Luther King talked of his dream of unity. Paul says it is no dream, it is a reality in the church.

Study 2
Ephesians 2:11–22

1. Describe the Gentiles' relationship with God and with the Jews (verses 11–12).
2. What has changed in these relationships (verses 13–15)?
3. What two purposes of Jesus' death are given in verses 15–16? What does this mean for relationships between Christians?
4. What do the metaphors in verse 19 tell us about the relationship between Christians?
5. Describe the picture given of the church in verses 20–22.
6. What does this mean for how we view other Christians, no matter how well we know them or how different they are from us?
7. How does the relationship between Christians described here differ from how we often picture it?
8. What effect should this have on our life together as a church? (Ephesians 4:2–3 offers some suggestions.)
9. Why is the unity of the church so important (see John 17:20–21)?

3 : Which way is up?

Ephesians 4:7–16

My daughter Cara would like to be an artist when she grows up. She enjoys all things arty and so it's an obvious conclusion for her to draw at the age of seven. My two sons aren't so sure what they want to be, but at five and three years old that isn't surprising. Isaac (the five-year-old) would like to be a builder, a writer, an explorer and 'something to do with dinosaurs'. When I ask him which of these he would pick, he simply replies, 'All of them, of course.' Silly me.

Imagine asking a church the same question: 'What would you like to be when you grow up?' What would the replies be? Of course, if you used those exact words they might think you were being a little patronizing, so imagine changing it to this instead: 'What does this church want to become?', or 'What is the goal for the life of this church?' Questions like this get at the heart of the *purpose of the church*, which is the topic for this chapter, and the subject of this passage from Ephesians.

Thinking about the purpose of the church is crucial for all of us involved in church life, because our purpose affects our actions. Our purpose guides how we spend our time. It controls our decisions. It influences our ethos and shapes our structures. This is well illustrated by Rick Warren, a pastor in the United Sates, in his popular book *The Purpose Driven Church*. The idea of the book is very simple really: Rick Warren outlines the aims of the church, and then he describes a structure and an organization that is designed to achieve those aims. And so it is a 'purpose driven church'. Its purposes drive and shape all that it does.

It's hardly rocket science, is it? In fact, put like that it might seem a pretty obvious thing to do. And yet many churches fail to do it. We usually assume that we will continue to do things the way they've always been done. And if we do think about changes, we rarely go back to our *purpose for existence*. For example, we might ask, 'How can we improve our Sunday services?' But we don't usually step back and ask, 'What's the aim of our Sunday services?' Or, 'How do our services fit into our overall purpose as a church?' The same would go for our house groups or cell groups.

Change for its own sake is not a good thing. We must never assume that because something has a long history it isn't the best way of doing things anymore. But it's worth asking the question: what's our purpose, and how can we best achieve it? It's worth asking that question even if in the end no changes are made, because that process will give us greater clarity in knowing why we do what we do. That will then affect our whole attitude and approach in doing those things. Our Sunday services may look identical to how they have always been, but we might all take part in a different way because we know what we are trying to achieve in them.

The big picture of purpose

If you asked people what the church exists to do, someone would probably say, 'It exists to glorify God.' And that's absolutely right; that is its most foundational purpose. In Ephesians 3:10 we read this: 'His intent was that now, through the church, the manifold wisdom of God should be made known to the rulers and authorities in the heavenly realms, according to his eternal purpose which he accomplished in Christ Jesus our Lord.'

Do you see God's purpose or intent there? He intends that his own manifold wisdom will be made known to the rulers and authorities in the heavenly realms (that is, to all of the supernatural powers of the universe). In other words, God wants everyone to know how wise he has been in his plans of salvation; how great is the gospel of Jesus Christ!

So how is his wisdom to be made known to everyone? Verse 13 says that it is 'through the church'. So the most foundational purpose of the church is to be a display of God's wisdom. We glorify him: we point to him and show how wonderfully wise and gracious he is. So the first part of the diagram looks like this:

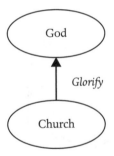

Diagram 4. The purpose of the church: part 1

But how do we glorify God? I'd suggest there are two ways. First, we glorify God by telling others about Jesus. In chapter 1 we looked at how we declare to the world what God has done (1 Peter 2:4–10). We also saw in that passage how the quality of our lives testifies to the world as well; and in chapter 2 we thought about how our unity in the church shows the world what God has achieved. So with our word about Jesus, in our godly lives, and in our unity together we witness to the world. And that's one way we glorify God. So we can add another part to the diagram.

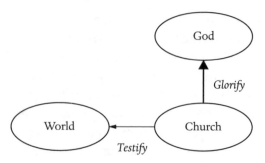

Diagram 5. The purpose of the church: part 2

But there's another way we glorify God, and this is the subject of the passage in Ephesians: the church is to 'build itself up in love' (4:16). In other words, the church is to *grow itself*. To show this on the diagram I've added an old-fashioned word: 'edify'. This simply means 'to build up'. And the building up of the church is the second way we glorify God. So the completed diagram looks like this:

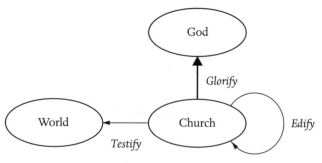

Diagram 6. The purpose of the church: part 3

The focus of the rest of this chapter is on the 'edify' bit of this diagram. By focusing on this part I don't want you to think that I don't believe in testifying to the world! I do. But as set out in the introduction, the main theme of this book is the church's 'internal life'. That's the purpose we're concentrating on.

Before we go on to think about how we 'edify' one another, I do want to make two further comments about the diagram. First, we must never become introverted and forget our purpose with regard to the world. And secondly, even in thinking about our internal life, it is vital to bear in mind that all we do is aimed not at ourselves but to glorify God.

So, let's think about our purpose: when we gather as church what are we up to?

We gather together to grow together

This passage in Ephesians 4 is all about a growing church. Paul uses two pictures to drive home the point he wants to make. The first is a picture of a building site. I used to pass a building site near where we used to live in North London. I enjoyed watching how the work progressed. First the area was cleared. Then trenches were dug and the foundations were set in place. Bricks were laid. Brick by brick, row by row, the building gradually rose higher and higher. Then one day when I went past I saw that the last slates had been laid on the roof and the building was finished.

Well, that's the picture Paul is conjuring up in verse 12 when he says 'so that the body of Christ may be built up'. The 'body of Christ' is the church, and Paul sees it like that building site, gradually moving towards completion. He's not thinking in terms of more people being added to the church, he's thinking of the building growing to be more like it is supposed to be. The church is supposed to be moving towards the finished product where everything is as it should be.

The second picture Paul uses is that of growing up into adulthood. My children enjoy looking through the special photo album we made for each of them. Each one starts with a picture of them when they were just a few minutes old. As they turn the pages, they see pictures of themselves starting to crawl, then walk, and so on. As I look over their shoulder, I'm reminded of how they have grown, of all the things they can do now that they couldn't then. But they've still got a way to go before they reach adulthood, and that's what Paul means in verse 15 when he says 'we will in all things grow up into him who is the Head, that is, Christ'. The church is to be growing towards maturity.

In verse 16, just in case we haven't got the point, Paul uses both terms again and mixes his pictures up: 'the whole body, joined and held together by every supporting ligament, grows and builds itself up in love'.

The church is to go on growing and being built; it's a dynamic entity that is ever changing. We are supposed to be different today from how we were this time last year. We are supposed to be growing to maturity, working towards finishing the building.

The finished article

So what does the finished building or the mature adult look like? According to verse 13 we are to keep on growing and building 'until we all reach unity in the faith and in the knowledge of the Son of God and become mature, attaining to the whole measure of the fulness of Christ'.

There are two things to note from this verse. First, there is unity in the faith and knowledge of the Son of God. In the last chapter, we saw how we have been united in Christ already, but there is now to be growth in seeing that unity lived out. This is growth in the way our relationships work. This is living out what Paul commanded back in verse 3: 'Make every effort to keep the unity of the Spirit through the bond of peace.'

Now our unity is only ever unity in the gospel and the person of Jesus (the 'faith' and the 'Son of God'). There is no other way to build unity than on this foundation. And so Paul is also thinking of growth in our understanding of the faith and the person of Jesus – more on that later. But he is not thinking simply of us each growing in our own personal understanding; he is thinking of growth in the unity between us that that understanding should bring.

Secondly, in becoming mature we are 'attaining to the whole measure of the fulness of Christ'. Perhaps you have seen what looks like a giant 'thermometer' standing in front of a church building to indicate how a fund-raising campaign is going. Over time, the red line moves higher and higher. Up at the top is the final amount they are aiming for. To understand what Paul is talking about in this verse, picture one of those thermometers with a mark at the top that says 'the fulness of Christ'. And imagine a church gradually filling up and up until we attain to that measure.

That measure isn't just Christ-likeness for each of us as individuals; it is a measure for the whole body – it is the church being what it's supposed to be given that it is Christ's body. When the church attains that measure it will have reached the point where it all functions as he wants it to, with all its parts working perfectly together. Thinking of a team sport can help us understand this better (football or rugby come to my mind as the best ones, but any team sport will do). Individual players in a team will naturally improve in their abilities and skills and as they do so we would say they were developing or growing. In the same way, we might talk about our individual growth as Christians, saying 'I'm growing in my relationship with God', or 'I'm growing in my Christian life.' But individual development isn't the whole picture. In team sports the big question is, 'How well does the whole team play, *as a team*?' In fact, all individual growth has to be seen in that context. If a player is thinking of development only in terms of their own skills, independent of everyone else, they've lost the plot, haven't they?

It's the same with the church. We do grow as individuals, but we can't think only in terms of the individual. The Christian life is a team sport; and your team is your church. Paul wants to see the church growing towards functioning as a perfect team.

A great deal of the New Testament letters to churches is to do with this issue. If you read just to the end of this letter to the Ephesians you'll see how Paul writes about sharing with each other, being kind and compassionate to each other, loving and forgiving each other; getting rid of any bitterness, or anger, or malice between us, and so on. His letter is all about how the church relates, not just about our individual relationship with God.

Now this is a challenge to us because this isn't how we usually think of growth. We usually think of growth in terms of our personal relationship with God. So if we get something out of a Sunday service or a small group, we say we're growing. Well, that is true, but Paul's picture here is so much bigger: he's concerned with the growth of the whole body in its unity and maturity.

All of this is part of what is meant by the word 'edify' in diagram 6. The church is to grow up in these ways. And that statement of our purpose raises some questions for us.

Do we have a desire to grow?

It is very easy to get into maintenance mode as a Christian. We are happy with our church and our place in it. We enjoy our meetings and what we do in them. Well, that's great, but are we looking to grow? Are we looking to be different this time next year? It might be two steps forward and one step back sometimes, but are we pressing on, or are we staying in our comfort zone?

One way to answer that question is by our prayers. In our prayers do we spend time asking God to build up the church and move it on towards maturity? It is helpful to take that central verse, verse 13, and use it to pray for your church. Write it out, stick it up somewhere and pray for growth.

Is this the direction we are heading in?

It is all too easy to focus on other things as the measure of growth. Imagine people are saying that they are really enjoying the Sunday services and small groups at your church, they think the atmosphere is great, and they are learning loads, gaining new insights and feeling challenged and encouraged, all at the same time! That would be great, really great. But it doesn't necessarily mean the church is growing in the way Paul described, because he is thinking about how the whole team is operating, not about individuals.

The problem is there aren't easy markers for this. If you are a church leader it is not easy to sit back and ask, 'How are we growing?' because it's to do with growth in the quality of relationships in church as well as growth in knowledge. It's not about numbers on rotas, but the quality of our care and love. It's not about the size of the budget but our willingness to bear with each other and forgive each other. You can't put a measure on that. But that is what our direction is to be. And so we have to ask, 'Is that my direction, is that where I'm heading, is that where I'm putting my energies?'

Can we achieve this any better?

It's very easy for churches to get into running certain events and programmes which, once established, manage to take on a life of their own and there is an expectation that they must be maintained. No doubt they were set up for good reasons, and most of them continue for good reasons as well, but we must ask the question: 'Can we change anything to achieve our purpose more fully?'

But we are getting ahead of ourselves here – to begin to answer that question we need to look at our second point. We have established that we gather together to grow together, but how does that growth happen?

We gather together to give to each other

To understand this point we need to look again at Ephesians 4:7–8:

> But to each one of us grace has been given as Christ apportioned it. This is why it says:
>
>> 'When he ascended on high,
>> he led captives in his train
>> and gave gifts to men.'

These verses tell us that Jesus is giving out presents. Jesus is handing out a little package of 'grace' to each one of us, to every member of the church.

The phrase in verse 8 is a quote from Psalm 68, a psalm about God rescuing his people from Egypt, and being victorious over his enemies. And Paul says that all of that is fulfilled in Jesus. He is the one who has rescued his people and he has now ascended on high in triumph and he has handed out gifts like the spoils of war.

So what are these gifts? Verse 11 says, 'It was he who gave some to be apostles, some to be prophets, some to be evangelists, and some to be pastors and teachers.'

Jesus gives people certain roles and the abilities to undertake them. Now the first two of these refers to the role of apostles and prophets in starting the church and in giving us the gospel. Back in Ephesians 2:20 Paul refers to the church being built on the foundation of the apostles and prophets. And the thing about a foundation is that you don't lay it again once it's already been laid.

Then Ephesians 3:5 adds to that in saying that God chose to reveal the truth of the gospel to certain people (apostles and prophets) like Paul, and they had the role of relaying that truth and so giving a foundation to the church. So it seems clear that the apostles and prophets are unique gifts for the church's formation and they are not ongoing gifts in the life of the church. If you are wondering about the gift of prophecy that is mentioned in 1 Corinthians 14, that clearly is an ongoing gift, but it is different from the type of prophecy mentioned in Ephesians.

After apostles and prophets come evangelists and pastors and teachers, and these are not foundational, they are ongoing. We are all to be evangelists in that we are all to pass on the message of the gospel, but God has given some people a special gift for the work of evangelism. That might be the street preacher, or it might be the mission-meeting speaker, it might be the person who can just get alongside others in friendships and speak effectively to them. Paul doesn't give details of how they will work, just that they are gifted in evangelism.

Now the way Paul refers to the pastors and teachers means he's most likely talking about one position rather than two: a pastor/teacher. This makes sense because elsewhere in the New Testament when church leaders are spoken of as overseers or pastors, we are told they have to be able to teach. This is the group responsible for the care and direction of the local church and the primary way they do that is through teaching.

So Jesus gives specific gifts for the formation of his church (apostles and prophets), for its extension (evangelists) and its care and growth (pastor/teachers). But that's not the way all the growth is going to happen! The church doesn't grow by a few gifted individuals doing all the work. This gifting is just the start of the process. Diagram 7 shows how the process works.

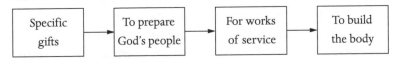

Diagram 7. The chain of equipping

In verse 12 Paul says that those specific gifts have been given to 'prepare God's people'. The idea is of equipping, or training for a certain purpose or task. The second part of the verse explains what the task is: to prepare God's people for 'works of service'. Put literally, it means for the work of ministry.

So the evangelist and the pastor/teacher are more like the conductors of an orchestra. They don't play all the instruments themselves, they get the whole orchestra playing well. They equip others so that everyone plays their part. Or you might find it more helpful to think of them like the manager of a football team who has to get all the players prepared for their task, and to get the team playing well together. That's what this group is to do.

And the purpose of it all is so that the body of Christ may be built up, so that the church may grow in the ways we have been thinking about. This is how that maturity is to be achieved. So do you see the flow of it? Jesus gives gifts, so that we will all work in ministry so that the body will grow to maturity. To make sure we get the point, Paul tells us the same things again in verse 16: 'From him the whole body, joined and held together by every supporting ligament, grows and builds itself up in love, as each part does its work.'

So as you look round at the faces of your church on a Sunday morning, what you are looking at is a self-building body. That group you see has the capacity to build itself up, to grow, as each part does its work. Each of them have different tools on the building site, each has a role to play, and as they get on with their work, the building moves towards completion.

Getting on with the job

The picture then is that the church grows by each member playing his or her part, prepared and conducted by the evangelists and pastor/teacher. In the next chapter, we will focus on the individual gifts we all have and how we are to use them in the life of the church, but before finishing this section I want to look at a role that we should all be playing. Paul writes: 'Instead, speaking the truth in love, we will in all things grow up into him who is the Head, that is, Christ' (verse 15). 'Speaking the truth in love' means teaching each other. Teaching truth to each other. One of the prime ways we will grow towards maturity is by growing in our understanding of God's truth, and in living it out together. And so we must teach each other. And we must do so lovingly.

Teaching each other in this way, and so building each other up, is normal church life. This is what should be happening week by week. Please don't think that teaching and instructing happens only in the sermons. Teaching hopefully does happen there very well. But Paul's commands in Ephesians 4 are about all of us teaching each other; all of us speaking the truth in love, or the whole body taking part in the works of service. So this is something everyone does. Or at least, something everyone should do.

It can happen wonderfully in Bible studies in small groups. As we each contribute to the discussion, our different perspectives can enrich and complement each other. So often you will be helped by something that someone else says in that discussion – and what you say will help others. You are speaking the truth in love; you are building each other up.

It can happen equally wonderfully in casual conversations between us. As we chat with each other, we can all bring truth to bear on the topic, or remind each other of something God has said. We can leave conversations having learnt something, or having taught something, or both. We are speaking the truth in love. Often, of course, we feel embarrassed about doing this; it can feel patronizing to mention a Bible passage. It can feel especially awkward if we feel we need to correct or even rebuke someone. But that's what speaking the truth involves, and that's what those other verses command. That's how the body will build itself up and grow.

Are you taking part?

So a last question: when you come to a Sunday service, or a small-group meeting, or you meet up with people from church, what should be in your mind? What do you hope to achieve; what do you want to happen? In other words, what's your *purpose*?

We need to come expecting to grow and learn ourselves, and expecting to take part in this maturing process. We will come wanting to receive from others in the body, come valuing how they will build us up. And we will come wanting to contribute ourselves, to give to others, to speak the truth in love to someone, to play our part, so that the body grows and builds itself up in love.

We will come wanting the church to move towards 'the whole measure of the fulness of Christ' because that's what we want the church to be when it grows up.

Study 3
Ephesians 4:7–16

1. In what different ways could you complete the following sentence: 'The church exists to ...'?
2. What gifts are referred to in verse 11? Describe these in your own words.
3. What purpose do these gifts have (verse 12)? How is this expressed again in verse 16?
4. What does this mean for our involvement in the church?
5. What is the purpose of the 'works of service' (verse 13)?
6. What is the church heading towards (verse 13)? Describe this 'perfect' church in your own words.
7. According to verse 15, one of the main ways we will grow is through 'speaking the truth in love'. How do you do this at your church? How might you do it better?
8. How should these purposes affect our own attitude to being involved in church?
9. How would you complete the following statement in the light of this passage: 'The church is going wrong if it is not ...'?

4 : What does it mean to belong?

1 Corinthians 12:4–27

In 1630, a guy called John Winthrop gave a great speech in an unusual place. He wasn't in a pulpit or on a conference platform. He was on the deck of a ship called the *Arbella*. The group he gave this speech to was sailing from England to start a new life in America and John Winthrop was the governor of the new colony they would found roughly where Boston is now. Before they landed he made a speech to his fellow colonists about his vision for the kind of society they would make. Towards the end of the speech he said this:

> 'We must be knit together as one man. We must entertain each other in brotherly affection ... We must delight in each other, make each other's conditions our own, rejoice together, mourn together, labour and suffer together, always having before our eyes our commission and community in the work, as members of the same body. So we shall keep the unity of the Spirit in the bond of peace.'

What a wonderful ideal for a new colony. A group with such solidarity that they rejoiced together and suffered together, and regarded themselves as bound together as one body, where each would play his or her part for the community.

Almost exactly 300 years later, in 1928, another speech was given which stands in rather stark contrast to Winthrop's. This time the speaker was Herbert Hoover who was about to become president of the United States. He finished his campaign for the presidency with what became known as the 'Rugged Individualism Speech'.

The title gives the game away really: 'rugged individualism' was how he saw the American spirit and ethos. His main concern was for free-markets and economics, but he still reflected an 'every-man for himself' ideal. Since then, the cult of the self-made man who is independent and free, who stands alone, has grown and grown. Winthrop's idealistic view of a united community has all but disappeared.

Like it or not, we who live in the West, whether in the United States or in Britain, live in a time where Hoover's view of individualism reigns, not Winthrop's idea of a community. The culture we have grown up in is a culture of individualism. The basic idea of individualism is simply the importance of the individual over anything else, like society or family. Individualism says that a person's own needs and wants come first, over and above everything else. Nowhere is this idea clearer than in advertising where we are told to 'Look out for Number One', or 'You're worth it.'

What this emphasis on individualism leads to is a culture of independence, self-sufficiency and freedom:

- *Independence*: you think of yourself as independent or separate from everyone else. You are your own person with no intrinsic bond with anyone else.
- *Self-sufficiency*: you can make it by yourself. In fact, dependence on others is seen as weakness, you must stand on your own two feet.
- *Freedom*: you are free of responsibility to others, your only responsibility is to yourself. You have no obligations to anyone else.

Now we all know that our culture isn't like that in its totality. People still act for the good of someone else, there is commitment in relationships and responsibility for others, and there is often a yearning for more of a community. But to some extent, individualism still taints us all.

But God doesn't believe in individualism. In fact, God's own being is made up of a community of three persons: Father, Son and Spirit. And God meant for us to live in similar community with each other. Of course, he created us as individuals, and we have our unique personalities and characters, but we are designed to live in community with him and each other. In the church God is re-creating a people who will live as he intended them to. Through the gospel people are reconciled to him and to each other; they are brought back to live with him as their God and king and brought back to live in the community of God's people.

What it means to belong to that community is the topic of this chapter.

To be united with each other

> The body is a unit, though it is made up of many parts; and though all its parts are many, they form one body. So it is with Christ. For we were all baptised by one Spirit into one body – whether Jews or Greeks, slave or free – and we were all given the one Spirit to drink (1 Corinthians 12:12–13).

Can you find the most frequently used word in these verses? It's the word 'one'. It actually occurs five times in two verses (verse 12 should start, 'The body is *one*'). Paul wants to emphasize unity – one Spirit who has made us all one body no matter how different we are. Paul's choice of metaphor for the church teaches us this: we are members of one body. It is as if we are different organs or limbs of the body. So the link between members of one church is as strong and as intimate as the link between your arm and your hand.

And Paul wants to stress that when someone is converted he or she is brought into this sort of close, united, body-part sort of relationship with other Christians. In verse 13, he says the Spirit has bound us together in one body, no matter who we are, no matter how different we are. Whether we are Jews or Greeks, whether we are slaves or free people, we have become bound to one another, united together as one body.

You may have spotted that I've said all this already in an earlier chapter. But it is worth repeating for two reasons: first, because it's so important, and secondly because I want us to think about what it means to belong. We often *talk* of the church being united as one body, but I'm less sure we actually *think* of the church like that. As we noted at the beginning of this chapter, we live in a very individualistic culture and we're naïve if we think we don't absorb some of that.

Picture a relationship

Think of how we view our relationship with other Christians. We usually think that we are connected together as Christians because of our common relationship with God. It's a bit like being polite to someone because you have a friend in common, or feeling you should take an interest in someone because you are involved in the same club. But this kind of attitude means that although we manage to speak about being 'united', at the same time we still think we are 'independent' of each other.

I used to go to a wine-tasting evening class (although I still know nothing about wine!). A typical class went like this: we listened to a talk, we tried some wines and discussed them, and then we went home. Everyone was very friendly and we got to know each other a bit over the weeks. But no-one there would have dreamt of saying that we were 'bound together like one body'! They would say, 'There's no real connection between us, we just share an interest in wine; we're just in the same group.'

But if we are honest, isn't that sometimes how we feel about the person we sit next to in church? Are we not in danger of thinking,

'There's no real connection between us, we just have a common interest in God; we're just in the same church'? It has to be said that the tendency to think that way is linked to the size of the church. In a large church, when you are sitting next to someone you have never met before, it can be very easy to think that way. It's less of a danger when you know everyone really well.

But large or small, it is still easy to operate a Christianized individualism in our thinking. We need to make a conscious effort not to think of ourselves as independent, but instead to think of ourselves as one. Becoming a Christian means a fundamental change in our relationship with each other – we don't just share something in common, we are part of the same body. We are bound together with everyone else, whether or not we know them well, or even like them very much. We haven't joined a voluntary club, we have become a family.

This is why Paul can say later in verse 26: 'If one part suffers, every part suffers with it; if one part is honoured, every part rejoices with it.' When your toe hurts, the rest of your body knows about it as well! Think of yourself as so connected with everyone else that what happens to them happens to you. As John Winthrop put it: we must 'make each other's conditions our own, rejoice together, mourn together'. So when you hear of things happening in other people's lives – illness or bereavement, a new job or a new baby – say to yourself 'We're united, and so I'm concerned; I must suffer with them or rejoice with them.'

Look round your church and say to yourself, 'One body'. Develop that mindset and combat the individualism that says we are independent.

To be responsible for each other

Chapter 12 in 1 Corinthians is best known not for the verses on unity we have just looked at, but for Paul's comments on gifting in the church. He doesn't just use the image of the body to convey the unity of relationship we have, he uses it also to convey the different *roles* we each have. Each Christian is a different part of the body: an ear, a hand, a foot and so on. And so we all have a different contribution to make. Paul makes this point clearly: 'There are different kinds of gifts, but the same Spirit. There are different kinds of service, but the same Lord. There are different kinds of working, but the same God works all of them in all men' (verses 4–6).

In these verses, Paul is saying roughly the same thing in three different ways: we all have different roles to play in the church but God is behind each of them. They all involve gifts from the same Spirit; they all involve serving the same Lord; they are all examples of the same God at work in us.

Some of the gifts listed here are much debated in the church today. Many books have been written on the subject, so I'm not going to add to that debate here. What I do want to do is look at the idea that God gives us each different gifts and works through us in different ways. Then we can think about what that means for belonging to a church.

Make your contribution

The purpose of the different gifts or roles we have is mentioned in verse 7: 'Now to each one the manifestation of the Spirit is given for the common good.' For each of us the Spirit works in different ways – we have different gifts – but they are all aiming at one thing: the common good (in other words, the good of the rest of the body). So you have a gift to use that is for the good of those who sit around you on a Sunday morning. You have a role to play in the building up of your church, and you have a responsibility to make your contribution.

Of course, sometimes you might not feel like using that gift. Well, that's how some people at Corinth felt as well. Look at verses 14–15: 'Now the body is not made up of one part but of many. If the foot should say, "Because I am not a hand, I do not belong to the body," it would not for that reason cease to be part of the body.'

Paul no doubt has in mind here the person who says 'They don't need me. My gifts aren't very important, I can't possibly make a valuable contribution.' It can be easy to feel like that at times.

But Paul responds to this by pointing out in verse 17 that the whole idea of a body is that it has lots of different parts; a body that was only an eye would be useless. 'In fact,' he goes on, 'God has arranged the parts in the body, every one of them, just as he wanted them to be' (verse 18). God has placed you in your role in the body. God has worked it all out and arranged it so that it works well. And that's why he has placed you in whatever your role is; he has chosen a tool for you and put it in your hand, whether it's a gift of teaching or prophecy, or showing mercy, or speaking wisdom. (By the way, the list of gifts in 1 Corinthians 12 is only a sample; we see more gifts mentioned in Romans 12:6–8 and 1 Peter 4:10–11.)

Whatever your role is, God has given it to you deliberately, and so you are most definitely needed. More than that, you have a responsibility to use your gifts, you have a unique contribution to make. In fact, the other people sitting around at church are depending on you to be exercising your gifts in their life. You have a responsibility to them so that they will grow, so that the whole church will grow. Use your gift for the common good. Or as Peter puts it: 'Each one should use whatever gift he has received to serve others, faithfully administering God's grace in its various forms' (1 Peter 4:10).

We have a responsibility to use our specific gifts, but in addition to that we all also have mutual responsibilities. These are things we all should be doing for each other. We looked at one of them in the last chapter – teaching one another or speaking the truth in love. But there are more:

- 'building each other up' (Romans 14:19: my translation);
- 'instruct one another' (Romans 15:14);
- 'have equal concern for each other' (1 Corinthians 12:25);
- 'serve one another' (Galatians 5:13);

- 'Carry each other's burdens' (Galatians 6:2);
- 'teach and admonish one another' (Colossians 3:16);
- 'encourage one another and build each other up' (1 Thessalonians 5:11);
- 'spur one another on . . . encourage one another' (Hebrews 10:24–25).

Do you see the picture? We have a responsibility to one another so that we help each other keep going in the Christian life, and grow in our relationship with God. If I was part of your church, I could walk up to you and tell you that you are responsible for encouraging me, for building me up, for teaching me and carrying my burdens, and so on. And all this in addition to your responsibility to use your specific gift in my life.

Now of course, it's not that any one person is solely responsible to do those things for any other person. But the church as a whole is responsible for each other's Christian lives, for making sure all of that list is happening. And every one of us is to be involved in that. There are to be no passengers in the church; we all have a job to do.

So we have a contribution to make: both in using our gifts, and in exercising those mutual responsibilities we all have. But how has individualism influenced the responsibility we have for each other? Individualism tells us we are free from such responsibility. The only person we are responsible for is ourselves. When we see someone struggling in their faith or going through hard times, we might say 'Someone ought to do something', but we don't often mean us. But God says, 'encourage one another', and 'carry each other's burdens'.

We've all heard the voice in our heads that says, 'Don't get involved; you don't know that person very well. You might say the wrong thing; anyway, other people will be looking after them. After all, you're too busy.' *Don't listen to that voice.* Listen to the voice that says, 'I'm united with this person and I have responsibilities here; this is my brother or sister and I'm going to get involved.' Look around your church and say to yourself, 'I've got a contribution to make here, I've got a responsibility to fulfil.' Fight against the tendency that says 'I'm free.'

Get involved with each other

We need to think a little about what this means in practice. How can we exercise this responsibility? How can we make sure we use our gifts in others' lives, caring for them, encouraging them and so on? First, it calls for interaction with each other. This will happen only if we are involved in each other's lives, rubbing shoulders with each other, spending time together.

In some areas of the United States, there are drive-in-churches. You sit in your car and tune in to the service on the radio. You sing the songs, pray the prayers, listen to the sermon. Then you can go home challenged and encouraged, and all without the hassle of having to talk to anyone else. All you need to do is wave at them through the window! I hope you recoil at the idea, given what the church is supposed to be. But here's the challenge: how easy is it for us to have a drive-in-church mentality in our own churches? We arrive, enjoy and leave, maybe even avoiding people so we won't have to chat.

Those involved in leading the services have a chance to teach or encourage everyone else. That's how they make their contribution, but it's limited to relatively few people. I do believe in services like that, but what bothers me is that they can give people the idea that the service is all there is to church. So I'm constantly telling people that if all they do is come to a Sunday service, their experience of church is defective.

We must interact with each other. A prime place for this is in small-group meetings. Only in that sort of context will you get to know people at a deeper level and be able to find out what is going on in their lives. And that's where you will be able to encourage them and pray for them and use your gifts in their lives. That's where you will teach each other as you share your insights in a Bible study, and that's where you will care for someone practically as a group. Small groups are the place where this happens best.

However, small groups are often seen as having Bible study as their sole purpose. Now I believe fervently that we should use small groups for Bible study, but if that's all, then many of the things on that list will not be done. The challenge for small-group leaders is to make the small group a place where people pray and encourage one another, care for each other, and so on.

Don't have a 'rota' mentality

Another way we avoid the richness of our contribution is that we think of service only as certain roles – usually stuff that you can put on a rota. So when someone is asked what they do at a church, they may say that they teach in Sunday School, they operate the overhead projector, or read in services, or set out the chairs, or belong to the welcome team, and so on. And all of that is great, and very important. It uses people's gifts and helps them to fulfil their mutual responsibilities. But some gifts can't be organized like that. What about the gift of encouragement? Does your church have an encouragement team? I doubt it, because you can't organize that gift in that way. If you have got the gift of encouragement, you just need to spend time with people, talking to them, and you will find yourself using your gift.

A focus on specific roles and rotas in the church can also mean that we feel we have done our bit if we've taken our turn at serving coffee. But our responsibilities can't be pinned down to rotas. That would be like having a rota that fulfilled all your responsibilities as part of a family. Imagine saying 'I've laid the table and I've emptied the bin, so I've fulfilled all my responsibilities here'! You just can't put it in those terms. So make sure to think beyond the contributions that can be put on a rota.

To be dependent on each other

There is one last area of what it means to belong to church. It comes in verses 21–22: 'The eye cannot say to the hand, "I don't need you!" And the head cannot say to the feet, "I don't need you!" On the contrary, those parts of the body that seem to be weaker are indispensable, and the parts that we think are less honourable we treat with special honour.'

The problem Paul is addressing in verse 21 is the attitude that makes people say, 'I don't need the hand, I'm an eye, and us eyes can get on very well by ourselves.' So the problem here is not feelings of inferiority (the subject of verse 14), but feelings of superiority.

Paul reminds us that no-one can say, 'I don't need anyone else', for we're all dependent on each other. Remember God has gifted each person so that the body will grow. That's how he's designed it; we need each other.

Admit your need

Individualism rears its ugly head again at this point. It tells us we are self-sufficient, we don't *need* anyone else, we can stand on our own two feet. Well, it's not just the Bible that tells us that's wrong; experience of life soon convinces us we need others too. But the influence of that individualistic thinking still filters through.

It shows itself in a number of ways. Let me expand. First, it causes us to reduce the number of people we think we need. We tell ourselves privately that it is only Mary, James and Andrew that we really need to help us in our Christian life, we're not dependent on everyone in the church, especially not Harry! Secondly, individualistic thinking leads us to restrict the number of gifts we think we need, limiting them to people who can encourage us and teach that we think we really need. Those are the gifts we want. We don't need those people who serve in other ways. And finally, we might convince ourselves that it's only when trouble comes that we need some help or comfort; in normal life we'll manage fine by ourselves, thank you very much.

Attitudes such as these simply water down the way the church is supposed to work. They are all modified versions of self-sufficiency, that says to some part of the body, 'I don't need you.'

But Paul says, 'The eye cannot say to the hand, "I don't need you".' And it can't say it to the leg, or the big toe, or any other part of the body. You can never look across your church meeting and say 'That person doesn't have a contribution to make', 'I'm not dependent on that person for anything.' You can never say 'I don't need you.'

On the contrary, Paul says we are dependent on others in the church. Our growth needs them, whether it is their teaching, comforting, serving, hospitality, word of insight or encouragement, we need it and our church needs it. So beware of thinking you are self-sufficient.

Some years ago, I used to meet up regularly with a man who, for a variety of personal difficulties, couldn't do very much in his church. He was the sort of person we might write off as being a drain on resources, not someone with a contribution to make. And I have to admit that I would have been tempted to think like that. I met up with him for his sake, not mine. But that person helped *me* grow, he challenged me in ways I'd never have imagined. That experience showed me that we can never say 'I don't need you.'

So will you admit your need of everyone else? Will you acknowledge that you are dependent on them? Look round your church and say, 'Each person here has a contribution to make.' Look round your small group and say, 'I need this group to keep me going as a Christian.'

Start a mutual appreciation society

Another implication of this is encouraging those around you to use their gifts. How? Simply by communicating that you appreciate what they contribute. Say, for example, that you have been wrestling with some issue in your life and one night in your small group someone says something during the Bible study that really helps. Or someone shares some struggle they have had and that reassures you. Or someone prays for you and you find it encouraging. Or over coffee someone says something that gives you a word of insight or wisdom, which helps you keep going or helps you grow.

Imagine if you tell that person how helpful they have been, that you appreciated their comment – not going over the top, not praising them, because the gifts all come from God – but simply saying, 'That was really helpful, thank you.' Or, 'I'm glad God has gifted you in this way.' If you say that, you will encourage them to continue commenting in Bible studies or sharing openly, or staying for coffee and chatting.

Compare that to what might happen if you don't say anything, and neither does anyone else. If they are never encouraged, never told they are appreciated, might they not be tempted to stop contributing, or sharing? And the same is true for any gift or service you can mention. That person should keep going of course, because we saw earlier that we are all to make our contribution. But a word of appreciation expresses our dependence, and encourages them.

Our dependence on each other means we should fan each other's gifts into flame; but so often we dampen them down by communicating the message that we are fine by ourselves. So start a mutual appreciation society. Or, to put it better, start a God-appreciation society that sees how he works through other people. Encourage each other, tell people you appreciate what they contribute.

So John Winthrop got it right. He thought of the colony they were founding as a church, and in his speech he was telling people what it meant to belong to church. If you turn back to the words of his speech at the start of the chapter, you'll see he summed it up brilliantly. And it's the opposite of rugged individualism. This is what it means to belong in the church: not to be independent but to be united with each other; not to be free but to be responsible for each other; not to be self-sufficient but to be dependent on each other.

Study 4
1 Corinthians 12:4–31

1. What do verses 4–7 tell us about gifts in the church? (Note: 'manifestation of the Spirit' in verse 7 is another way of talking about gifts that the Spirit gives.)

2. What point is Paul making in verses 12–13? What difference does this make to how we view ourselves and others in the church?

3. What problem is Paul speaking about in verses 15–17? How does he answer it in verses 18–20? Where are we prone to make this mistake ourselves?

4. What different problem is he addressing in verse 21? How does he answer it in verses 22–26? Where are we prone to make this mistake ourselves?

5. What attitude should we have to the contribution of others in the church? What attitude should we have to our own contribution in the church?

6. 1 Corinthians 12 focuses on our individual gifting. However, there are also more general responsibilities we have for each other. List any commands you can think of that involve the words, 'one another' or 'each other' (for example, 'Love one another').

7. How would you summarize these responsibilities we have for each other? Which of them would you rather avoid? Why?

8. What will this mean for your role in the life of your church? What will it mean for the life of your small group?

5 : Concrete love

Romans 12:3−21

Reading a newspaper a while ago I was struck by the phrase 'liquid love'. It was the title of a book by a sociologist called Zygmunt Bauman. The picture on the cover was of a beach with a large heart drawn in the sand and the tide was coming in. Along with the title, that picture seemed to suggest a type of 'love' that was rather temporary – the heart in the sand would be soon washed away leaving no trace that it had ever been there.

The general idea of Zygmunt Bauman's book is this: we want relationships; we want the togetherness and companionship that they bring; we want to express and receive love. But at the same time, we don't want the burden that comes with commitment. We certainly don't want to be trapped, caught up in other people's problems. That's the tension we feel. We want closeness with other people so we can have a sense of community and belonging, but we want to keep our distance so people don't engulf us or impose on us.

And so Bauman coined the phrase 'liquid love'. We want our love to be able to flow where we want, rather than being pinned down, and set in place. We want some ties to other people but we don't want those ties to be too tight. We would like to be able to undo the knots if ever we wanted to.

This attitude can be seen all around us. Read any agony-aunt column and you'll find comments about being careful not to over-commit. Or advice about how to withdraw from a friendship you no longer find rewarding. Or suggestions on how to handle a friend who is too demanding. In other words, how to keep your love *liquid*.

So what is our love as Christians supposed to look like? Christians are supposed to be loving people – there are numerous commands that tell us that, including the one in this passage from Romans that is the focus of this chapter. In fact, the topic of love is so important for Christians and for church life that I'm devoting two chapters to it. This command in Romans 12 is a kind of bridge between love and what we have been thinking about church already.

What Paul says in this passage is that living as a Christian means loving each other and the world around us. But it's not to be liquid love. In fact, the title I've given this chapter tells you that it is to be the opposite – concrete love.

First, I want to recap on what we already know.

We belong to each other

'Just as each of us has one body with many members, and these members do not all have the same function, so in Christ we who are many form one body, and each member belongs to all the others' (Romans 12:4–5).

We have already looked at this 'body' picture of the church in the last chapter, but Paul adds something extra in the Romans passage. We are like different parts of a body, intimately bound together, and so Paul says 'each member belongs to all the others'. Literally, we are all members *of* each other.

So here we are back to thinking about the closeness of

relationship between Christians. We belong to each other. If you were in my church I could walk up to you and say, 'You belong to me'; or rather I should say, 'You belong to everyone else here.' You might think I was weird if I did so, but that actually illustrates how weird this is. Paul is talking about a closeness here that is way beyond friendship or team spirit – we are forged together in such a way that we belong to each other.

Most people want a sense of belonging. They want to feel part of a group, to be known and loved in a community. You may remember the old TV series *Cheers* about a mixed group of people who met up in a bar. The words of its theme tune are about going somewhere, 'Where everybody knows your name, and they're always glad you came.' It might be a bit cheesy, but it is what we want. And in today's broken and fractured society we need it more than ever.

The reason we want that sense of belonging is because that is how God made us to function. He made us to be relational. And the breaking of relationships, and the hurt and loneliness that comes with them, are due to the fall into sin. So our desire for true community is a great desire, a good and godly desire. And it's a desire that is met in the church. In the church we truly belong to each other.

The only problem is, we belong rather more fully than we might like. To the modern man or woman working on the 'liquid love' model, this stuff about belonging sounds almost suffocating. Remember, with liquid love we don't want the knots that tie us to other people to be too tight. But Paul pictures the opposite extreme: we are bound together with knots that can't be undone. We can't say, 'I'd like a bit of freedom now, I'd like to undo my ties to these other people.' We belong to each other.

Along with that we don't even get to choose those we are tied to. We're bound together with anyone else who is in Christ. There is an old Christian song that begins, 'Bind us together Lord'. One of the lines asks God to bind us together 'with cords that cannot be broken'. I never liked singing that song because there were lots of people around who I didn't particularly want to be tied to in any way, let alone with unbreakable cords. No-one told me the reality was actually even more daunting than the song suggested: there was no need to ask God to bind us together in such a way at all, because he'd already done it. I was bound with unbreakable cords to all these people already. If you are a Christian, you are too. We belong to each other.

Think this way

Paul wants the church in Rome, and us, to grasp that idea of belonging because there's a danger we must avoid. See verse 3: 'For by the grace given me I say to every one of you: Do not think of yourself more highly than you ought, but rather think of yourself with sober judgment, in accordance with the measure of faith God has given you.'

People have debated the meaning of that phrase 'the measure of faith God has given you'. It sounds as if God has gone round with a ladle and measured out different amounts of faith to each person, and Paul is saying we should think of ourselves according to how much we have been given.

But I don't think that is how we are meant to understand this phrase. For instance, it leads to some weird questions: Exactly what should I think about myself if I have been given a lot of faith? What should I think if I've been given a little? And how do I know how much faith I've been given anyway?

There is another way of understanding Paul's words which makes more sense in the context. After all, this stuff about belonging to each other in verses 4–5 is an explanation of verse 3, so they must fit together somehow. I think the way they fit is this: the measure of faith isn't like a measuring jug that God fills up to different levels, it's a standard by which to measure ourselves, which is the same for all of us.

It's like setting your watch in accordance with the standard of Greenwich Mean Time. We are to 'set' our thinking in accordance with this standard – the standard (or measure) of faith. Paul wants us to think of ourselves in accordance with *the* faith, that is who we are in Christ. In other words, think of yourself knowing that we are bound together as members of one body.

He warns us of the danger we face if we don't see ourselves in this way – we will be inclined to think more highly of ourselves than we ought (verse 3). We put ourselves on a pedestal and our thinking about ourselves is enlarged. We all get 'big head' syndrome.

Most groups of people who do things together end up dividing into some sort of hierarchy. And if we are part of that group we might ask ourselves 'Where am I on the ladder?' And we all like to place ourselves a fair way up it. What Paul is saying here is, 'Don't think like that; set your thinking in accordance with who you are in Christ.' In other words, 'Don't even ask that question in the church – there isn't a ladder, we are like a body, we are bound together with everyone else.'

If we are honest, most of us would admit we are prone to thinking of ourselves more highly than we ought. That might be because of particular gifts or roles we have, or because of our background. But Paul says, 'Don't think like that – think of yourself as belonging to each other.'

Body life

Thinking like that is important because how we think affects the way we live. And Paul describes the results. If we remember we belong to each other, we will live as a body.

See verses 6–8:

> We have different gifts, according to the grace given us. If a man's gift is prophesying, let him use it in proportion to his faith. If it is serving, let him serve; if it is teaching, let him teach; if it is encouraging, let him encourage; if it is contributing to the needs of others, let him give generously; if it is leadership, let him govern diligently; if it is showing mercy, let him do it cheerfully.

As in the last chapter, the picture of the body isn't just about our being bound together; it is also to do with the different roles or gifts we each have.

In verse 6, the phrase about using the gift of prophecy in proportion to a person's faith is one that, like the phrase in verse 3, is difficult to understand. It seems to say that if I've got a lot of faith, then I can *really* prophesy, but if I don't, then I'd better be careful! Again this raises questions as to how I know how much faith I've got, and what is the right 'proportion' to what I've got. Actually the word 'his' isn't there, it just reads 'use it in proportion (or accordance) to *the* faith'. That simply means prophesying only stuff that is right and true – stuff that fits with *the* faith.

But the main point of what Paul is saying is, 'Whatever your gift is, get on with using it.' Imagine you get a work party together to do some DIY. You walk round at the start and give some people paintbrushes, some screwdrivers, others hammers, and so on. And then you say, 'Whatever tool you've got, get on and use it.' Paul's cry here is like that: 'If your gift is serving, get serving; if it's encouraging, get encouraging.' The church is like a ship where the only people on board are the crew, and they all have a job to do, they all have responsibilities.

Now 'liquid love' would shy away from such responsibilities. Liquid love would say, 'I don't want to get too involved, because people might start to expect stuff from me.' Liquid love would have us be wary of over committing, because we might get drawn in more than we want. Liquid love would hide that gift, or at least use it only sparingly. Liquid love would want the option of pulling out of using that gift whenever it wanted. After all, it might become inconvenient.

But Paul says we belong to each other, like a body, and so we are to live as a body. That is not supposed to mean we can never stop serving somewhere in church. People's circumstances change and churches need to be flexible. But you still see the challenge. We will tend to want to keep our distance and commit only as much as is convenient; Paul says we belong to each other, and so we are committed whether we like it or not.

Family life

> Love must be sincere. Hate what is evil; cling to what is good. Be devoted to one another in brotherly love. Honour one another above yourselves. Never be lacking in zeal, but keep your spiritual fervour, serving the Lord. Be joyful in hope, patient in affliction, faithful in prayer. Share with God's people who are in need. Practise hospitality (verses 9–13).

There's a mixture of things in those verses, but the central idea is living as a loving family together. It begins in verse 9 with 'Love must be sincere', meaning without any hypocrisy or pretence. There's to be no play-acting at love in church; there's to be no lip-service to the idea of love. Unfortunately too many people can tell stories of churches that have given the impression that they were places of love, but the reality was far different.

Alison's story is a case in point. She was due to go into hospital for a major operation. She was to stay in hospital for a week of so, and then spend several months at home convalescing. She was assured of the prayers and support of the church before she went. Someone kindly gave her a lift to the hospital, but once there, no-one visited or organized a lift home (she struggled home on the bus!). During her convalescence no-one visited her. In fact, she saw no-one from church until she was well enough to get to church again by herself, where she was greeted with the casual comment, 'You haven't been here for a while have you?'

Such an appalling lack of love – hypocritical love – left Alison wounded and hurting, unsure whom she could trust and rely on in the church. Paul is saying that there should be none of that; love must be a reality, not simply a nice idea we talk about. We should shun all such ugly perversions of love and cling instead to what is right and true (second half of verse 9).

Verse 10 is even stronger: 'Be devoted to one another in brotherly love', or better still, 'family' love. We have seen that we are brothers and sisters in God's family. Well, says Paul, live out that family love together. This involves honouring others above ourselves (second half of verse 10). That is, thinking of others as more important than us and so doing what would be good for them. Thinking of their needs and concerns above our own.

It will mean sharing with God's people who are in need (verse 13). When someone's not so well off financially or materially, it will mean putting your hand in your pocket, or sharing something you have with them. That might be your car, your food, your energy or your time. Whenever you come across a fellow Christian who is needy in some way, this family love asks, 'How can I help?' or 'What do I have that I can share with that person?'

This means practising hospitality (verse 13). We are to welcome each other into our homes; more than that, we are to welcome each other into our lives. It doesn't matter how different you are, because you are family. This is a picture of a group of people who know that they are bound together and belong to each other, and so they are devoted to each other.

Liquid love, of course, would be wary of this; it would be careful about over committing. After all, who knows where that might lead you, who knows what burdens might come your way. Liquid love would say, 'Keep those bonds loose.' But Paul would say, 'You can't keep them loose, you are bound together, so be devoted to each other.'

And as a result, the church is the place where there will be true community. There will be supportive relationships. There will be care and concern for each other. Liquid love wants some of that without the commitment, the benefits without the cost, if you like. But it can't be done. True community and true commitment to people go hand in hand.

I was once invited to speak at a weekend away for a group from a large city-centre church. It was a similar sort of church to the one where Alison's story took place. Large churches are harder places to establish true community. It's easier for people to slip through the cracks and not be noticed. Someone on that weekend away began telling the story of a woman called Julie who had been in her small group. Julie had moved to that city relatively recently, and didn't know anyone there. She'd been in this small group but it was then disbanded. She fell ill and was hospitalized for a whole summer. And as the person began the story, I thought it was going to be another lack-of-love horror-story.

But she went on to say that even though the group was disbanded, someone took the initiative to get them to discuss what they could do. They ended up organizing *daily* visits and did loads of other practical stuff for her both in hospital and once she got home. Isn't that wonderful? Isn't that what you would want to find in a church? But didn't that take commitment and some sacrifice by the rest of the group? There's concrete love for you.

God's people in the world

We have been thinking about love in the church; that is where we love 'one another' with this family love. But I want to finish this chapter by thinking about how we love people who aren't in the church. We know that the second greatest commandment is 'Love your neighbour as yourself' (Mark 12:31). And we know that Jesus wants us to think of anyone and everyone as our neighbour (see Luke 10:27–37). In other words, we should love those around us.

In fact, we need to go further than that; we are also to love our enemies. In Romans 12, Paul is probably picking up on those words of Jesus in the Sermon on the Mount (Matthew chapters 5 – 7). In that sermon Jesus said, 'Love your enemies and pray for those who persecute you' (Matthew 5:44). So, Paul says in Romans 12:14, 'Bless those who persecute you; bless and do not curse.'

Reflect God's love

The idea Jesus was working out here was this: as God's people in the world, the church is to reflect God's attitude to the world. That is, we are to reflect his love to the world. Jesus said, 'He causes his sun to rise on the evil and the good, and sends rain on the righteous and the unrighteous' (Matthew 5:45). In other words, God is equally kind and generous in supporting life no matter how people live. So, he says, you should reflect the same attitude – you ought to love your enemies as well as your friends. As God's people, reflect God's attitude.

That's the point that Paul is picking up here. We are to reflect God's love to everyone. That leads to some pretty startling conclusions. It means expressing love to people, no matter what they do to you. If that last sentence didn't strike you, worry you and challenge you, read it again.

See how Paul puts it in verses 17–18 of our main passage: 'Do not repay anyone evil for evil. Be careful to do what is right in the eyes of everybody. If it is possible, as far as it depends on you, live at peace with everyone.'

Paul knows that people will wrong us in some way; that is, they will do 'evil' to us. It might be big stuff, like people persecuting us for being a Christian. It might be minor stuff, like a neighbour playing their music too loudly, or someone making a sharp move against us in business. But whatever it is, whatever its motivation, we need to know how to respond.

Paul says, 'Don't retaliate. Live at peace with people, as far as it is down to you – don't stir it up.' In other words, be careful of standing on your rights so much that you start picking a fight. Be careful to do what's right in the eyes of everyone. That is trying to live in such a way that no-one could accuse you of being in the wrong, or responding badly.

Paul tells us to go beyond just not retaliating. He tells us to bless people instead. That means to pray for good things for them, to call down God's blessing on them, even when you might feel like calling down his curse. We see the same thing again in verse 20:

'If your enemy is hungry, feed him;
   if he is thirsty, give him something to drink.
In doing this, you will heap burning coals on his head.'

It's important here to note that he doesn't mean that being kind to someone is the best way of getting your own back at them! That would run against all he's saying here. That phrase 'heap burning coals on their head' refers to the shame that this sort of action can bring. When someone attacks you, you can show them that what they are doing is wrong by the way you act to them. You respond in love and they end up burning with shame as a result.

I heard recently of a church in Uganda. When it started it was very small, just a handful of people, and it suffered persecution from the village it was in. People who went to the church were beaten up. Imagine that happening at your church. Picture someone you know and imagine they were beaten up just because they came to your church. How would you react? What would you do?

If you're anything like me, your blood would be boiling. You would feel like retaliating if you could. You would hardly be thinking kind thoughts to whoever was responsible. But Paul says 'Do not take revenge, my friends, but leave room for God's wrath' (verse 19). Leave the justice stuff to God. And he says 'Do not repay anyone evil for evil' (verse 17).

Perhaps, then, we should just ignore it, stay neutral. Perhaps this church in Uganda should just keep its head down, and not get involved in the community but focus in on itself. But Paul says, 'Bless those who persecute you' (verse 14), and 'If your enemy is hungry feed him' (verse 20). You can't just turn your back, you have to reflect God's love to people, no matter what they do to you. Even if they have made themselves your enemies.

So what did that church in Uganda do? They started a child sponsorship scheme and a school. They did a huge amount to love their community and to care for the people there. And as time passed the persecution gradually stopped. I don't know of course, but I wouldn't be surprised if the people involved in that persecution felt ashamed for what they had done. What a wonderful example of Paul's words in verse 21: 'Do not be overcome by evil, but overcome evil with good.'

So what sort of disputes or conflict are you involved in? Is there some nasty coffee-room gossip about you, or is there a family argument? Is there a legal wrangle or an argument with a neighbour? What is your attitude to whoever it is that is wronging you? It's not easy, but God calls us to love them – to bless them, to care for them.

What about 'liquid love' here? Well, liquid love wouldn't even ask the question; it would have left long ago. It questions how much to love friends, never mind enemies. The world will find this kind of behaviour very strange, abnormal even. But it will speak volumes to the world about the love of God.

Study 5
Romans 12:3–21

Verses 3–8
1. How does Paul want people in the church to think about themselves and their relationship with other Christians?
2. What does this mean for what we contribute to the life of the church?
3. When do we least want to get involved in church life? Why?

Verses 9–13
4. What sort of attitudes and actions does Paul want in the church?
5. Which of these is most counter-cultural?
6. Which of these do you want to grow in yourself? In order to do that, what will you do differently this week?

Verses 14–21
7. How does Paul want Christians to behave towards those outside the church?
8. How should you respond when you are treated badly?
9. What situations have you been in where these verses are especially relevant? Is there anything you would do differently?

6 : All you need is love

How would people down your street describe the people at your church? If asked for an opinion on you as a group, what would they say? Or how would they describe Christians generally? We know what non-Christians were saying about one church a long time ago, because a guy called Tertullian who lived in the second century quotes some of the things they were saying. What do you think they said? 'See how they love one another ... See how they are ready even to die for one another.'

What those people outside the church were referring to was the practical care and compassion they saw in the church. They were amazed at the extent and the degree of love being expressed between Christians. These people laid lives on the line for each other: 'See how they are ready even to die for one another.'

Love between Christians is thought to be a significant factor in the spread of the gospel. It was seen in the care given to those in the church who were poor or widowed or orphaned, in days when people in these situations would simply starve. It was seen in the visits made to Christian brothers and sisters in prison, or the way they tended those who were sick. They shared their possessions with each other. Onlookers could tell that these people were followers of Jesus Christ simply by the quality of care there was between them.

We shouldn't be surprised really. All those Christians were doing was following through on what Jesus had told them to do. Jesus said: 'A new command I give you: Love one another. As I have loved you, so you must love one another. By this all men will know that you are my disciples, if you love one another' (John 13:34–35).

They were living out that command – love one another as I have loved you. Today it seems we can sometimes look on it not so much as a command but as an optional extra. Think of buying a car. You can get the basic model or you can have the optional extras – the computerized navigation system, cruise control, leather seats, multi-CD changer. The basic model gets you around OK but the optional extras turn it into a luxury experience.

Sometimes we think about church in a similar way. There is the basic model, with sermons, songs and Bible studies. But 'love' is like an optional extra; we can have it if we've got the time and energy. But if we don't have it, that's OK, it will still work fine. But according to Jesus, 'love' in the church is as basic as a chassis is to a car. This is fundamental to who we are, it's part of what it means to be church.

To get a feel for how important this love is in the life of the church, look at the number of verses which talk about it:

'My command is this: *Love* each other as I have loved you. Greater love has no-one than this, that he lay down his life for his friends' (John 15:12);

'This is my command: *Love* each other' (John 15:17);

'Let no debt remain outstanding, except the continuing debt to *love* one another, for he who loves his fellow-man has fulfilled the law' (Romans 13:8);

'Do everything in *love*' (1 Corinthians 16:14);

'You, my brothers, were called to be free. But do not use your freedom to indulge the sinful nature; rather, serve one another in *love*' (Galatians 5:13);

'The entire law is summed up in a single command: "*Love* your neighbour as yourself"' (Galatians 5:14);

'May the Lord make your *love* increase and overflow for each other and for everyone else, just as ours does for you' (1 Thessalonians 3:12);

'Now about brotherly love we do not need to write to you, for you yourselves have been taught by God to *love* each other. And in fact, you do *love* all the brothers throughout Macedonia. Yet we urge you, brothers, to do so more and more' (1 Thessalonians 4:9–10);

'And let us consider how we may spur one another on towards *love* and good deeds' (Hebrews 10:24);

'Keep on *loving* each other as brothers' (Hebrews 13:1);

'If you really keep the royal law found in Scripture, "*Love* your neighbour as yourself," you are doing right' (James 2:8);

'Now that you have purified yourselves by obeying the truth so that you have sincere *love* for your brothers, *love* one another deeply, from the heart' (1 Peter 1:22);

'*Love* the brotherhood of believers' (1 Peter 2:17);

'... live in harmony with one another; be sympathetic, *love* as brothers, be compassionate and humble' (1 Peter 3:8);

'Above all, *love* each other deeply, because *love* covers over a multitude of sins' (1 Peter 4:8);

'This is the message you heard from the beginning: We should *love* one another' (1 John 3:11);

'Dear friends, since God so loved us, we also ought to *love* one another' (1 John 4:11);

'I ask that we *love* one another' (2 John 1:5).

It is not unreasonable to suggest that the defining word you should want to hear from your non-Christians friends is that your church is a place of love.

What sort of love?

We need to start by thinking about the type of love we are to show. John 15:12, which I quoted above, says we are to love each other *as* Christ has loved us. We can see the same point in these verses:

'. . . live a life of love, just as Christ loved us and gave himself up for us as a fragrant offering and sacrifice to God' (Ephesians 5:2);

'This is how we know what love is: Jesus Christ laid down his life for us. And we ought to lay down our lives for our brothers' (1 John 3:16).

Jesus defines loves for us in his death on the cross. And so he sets a model of how we are to love each other. Our love is to be patterned on his. So how did Jesus love us?

'No matter what' love

Jesus loved us when we didn't deserve it; so our love is to be *unconditional*. It is not to turn on what someone does for us. It is not dependent on what our background is with that person, how much we like them, or how well we know them. It is not to vary on what our future is with that person, whether we will even see them again. In fact, this love is to be there, even when that person has ignored us, offended us or hurt us. That's an easy thing to write, but I am all too aware what a hard thing that is for us to do. But that is what Jesus did for us, and he says, 'Love each other as I have loved you.'

'Painful' love

Jesus loved us at immense personal cost; so our love too is to be sacrificial if need be. It is not to have limits of quantity or quality. There are to be no boundaries to it. It cost Jesus his life, and he asks that we love in the same way. As a result, we should expect our love to be painful sometimes. I am not saying that it will be all doom and sadness. Not at all. In fact, I think we will find loving people sacrificially a fulfilling and joyful experience. But it will cost us. It will cost our time, our energy and our money. It will drain us emotionally or physically. Remember the comment from Tertullian, 'See how they are ready even to die for one another.'

Pictures of love

What follows is a series of passages from the New Testament which give us examples of this sort of love in practice. I hope they will stimulate us in thinking about how we 'live a life of love' in our churches.

Share it around

All the believers were together and had everything in common. Selling their possessions and goods, they gave to anyone as he had need. Every day they continued to meet together in the temple courts. They broke bread in their homes and ate together with glad and sincere hearts, praising God and enjoying the favour of all the people. And the Lord added to their number daily those who were being saved (Acts 2:44–47).

All the believers were one in heart and mind. No-one claimed that any of his possessions was his own, but they shared everything they had. With great power the apostles continued to testify to the resurrection of the Lord Jesus, and much grace was upon them all. There were no needy persons among them. For from time to time those who owned lands or houses sold them, brought the money from the sales and put it at the apostles' feet, and it was distributed to anyone as he had need. Joseph, a Levite from Cyprus, whom the apostles called Barnabas (which means Son of Encouragement), sold a field he owned and brought the money and put it at the apostles' feet (Acts 4:32–37).

I want us to look at two acts of love here: giving to those who are in need and sharing possessions.

First, giving to those who are in need. There was a generous giving up of financial resources for the sake of others. This is an example in practice of what John speaks about later in his letter: 'If anyone has material possessions and sees his brother in need but has no pity on him, how can the love of God be in him? Dear children, let us not love with words or tongue but with actions and in truth' (1 John 3:17–18).

This kind of love will have an impact today. Churches should care for those in financial need. This will usually be overseen by the leadership of the church, following the pattern in Acts of putting the money in a central 'pot' and the leaders distributing it as is needed. When someone in our churches is in financial difficulty some of the church funds will often be used to help. So we should think of what we give to the church as going, at least in part, to others in the church.

But this raises a lot of issues: What if the people in question have not been very sensible with their money? How much do you give them? How poor do people have to be before you help? Do we go and ask people how they are financially, or wait for requests?

Consider three situations. The first one concerns a couple, Barbara and Neil, who seem to be struggling. When Neil had to be off work with long-term illness, a crisis loomed. However, it was relatively well known that they weren't great at handling their money. For example, when they were given a gift recently they had immediately bought an expensive new computer. What should the church do?

The second situation is the result of bereavement. The death of Sheila's husband meant a significant drop in income and lots of people in the church were concerned how she was doing financially. They were ready to help, but didn't know if it was needed. But everyone was too embarrassed to ask for fear of causing offence. What should happen?

The third concerns Ian and Wendy, the odd ones out in the church. No-one there was particularly rich, but everyone was comfortable financially, except Ian and Wendy. Their car was a decade older, and their house was a size smaller. But they just about managed OK. Should the church help at all?

It would be easy to be paralyzed by these difficult questions and end up doing nothing. But I hope you see that doing nothing simply isn't an option. We will certainly make mistakes, but we need to wade in and do something. And as we do so, we will grow in wisdom as to how to love sensitively.

In case you were wondering, in the three situations I mentioned the following happened. The church did give some financial help to Barbara and Neil but they also tentatively suggested paying for a consultation with an advisor who helps people manage their own finances. Eventually someone explained to Sheila that people were concerned for her finances and asked if she needed any help. She was touched by the concern, rather than offended, but she was managing fine. Having considered Ian and Wendy, the leadership decided not to offer any help, but to keep a careful eye on how they were doing.

The second act of love we see in these passages in Acts is sharing of possessions: 'No-one claimed that any of his possessions was his own, but they shared everything they had.' People didn't think of what they owned as theirs so much as belonging to the family – the church. What a different view of possessions!

This has resulted in some churches setting up 'sharing schemes' of different sorts. There will be a place for that in many settings. But in all settings there should be the spontaneous sharing of what we own. That will often involve lending stuff – and lending it to whoever needs it, rather than only to those we know or like. Some people have gone so far as to insure their car for all drivers, so that they can lend it to whoever needs it in the church. Others make space available in their house for regular visitors, even when they don't know them very well.

My wife and I were in the United States for a work exchange for a few months. While we were there we went to a church. On our last Sunday at church before we went on a holiday and then back home I was talking to Bill. He was asking about our holiday plans and I explained the long tour we had in mind. Then he asked what car we had, and when I explained we were renting one, he replied, 'We've got two, you must borrow one of ours.' I'd only met this guy once before and only for an afternoon. So with usual British reserve I replied, 'No really we mustn't; it's very generous of you, but there's no need.' I'll never forget his reply. He looked at me kindly and said, 'But we're family Graham, we should share things in the family.' 'You're right', I replied, 'We are family – thank you very much.'

Breach of love

In those days when the number of disciples was increasing, the Grecian Jews among them complained against the

Hebraic Jews because their widows were being overlooked in the daily distribution of food. So the Twelve gathered all the disciples together and said, 'It would not be right for us to neglect the ministry of the word of God in order to wait on tables. Brothers, choose seven men from among you who are known to be full of the Spirit and wisdom. We will turn this responsibility over to them and will give our attention to prayer and the ministry of the word.'

This proposal pleased the whole group. They chose Stephen, a man full of faith and of the Holy Spirit; also Philip, Procorus, Nicanor, Timon, Parmenas, and Nicolas from Antioch, a convert to Judaism. They presented these men to the apostles, who prayed and laid their hands on them.

So the word of God spread. The number of disciples in Jerusalem increased rapidly, and a large number of priests became obedient to the faith (Acts 6:1–7).

This passage describes a problem in the church between the Greek and Hebrew Christians. The church was rightly looking after the widows in the congregation – an act of practical love. But the Greek widows were being overlooked. We are not told why, just that they were. The twelve apostles who were the leaders of this Jerusalem church rightly decided they shouldn't get involved themselves, because their specific responsibilities lay elsewhere. This passage is often used as an example of how the priority for leaders is prayer and ministry of the word. It does clearly teach that, and we must not burden our elders and ministers with practical tasks that distract them from teaching us the Bible clearly and praying for the church.

But what is not so often emphasized is that while they did keep that as their priority, they didn't ignore the problem. You see, they could have said to themselves, 'This isn't our area, it's a shame it's happening, but we musn't get distracted.' But that wasn't their attitude. Instead, their thinking was more like this: 'This is significant, people are being overlooked, this is a breach of the principle of love, and so we must make sure something is done. We can't do it ourselves so we must put some good people on the case.'

Likewise today, we may come across examples of a breach of love. Someone lives alone and can't get out much, but no-one visits. Another person struggles to get to the shops, but no-one offers to take her. A single mum or dad is finding that life with the kids is wearing but no-one offers to look after them, even occasionally. And on it goes. The principle of love is breached because of people's busyness, lack of awareness, prejudice, and many other reasons. But whenever we discover a breach of love we should try to remedy it. It might not end up being our job, but it doesn't mean we shrug our shoulders. The church leadership especially should have the attitude of wanting to find people whose gift it is to help in such situations.

Get in their shoes

> Keep on loving each other as brothers. Do not forget to entertain strangers, for by so doing some people have entertained angels without knowing it. Remember those in prison as if you were their fellow prisoners, and those who are ill-treated as if you yourselves were suffering (Hebrews 13:1–3).

The author tells them to keep on loving and then gives two examples. The first is to provide hospitality to strangers and the second is remembering those in difficult situations. I'd like us to think about the second of these. At the time passage was written, some Christians were being persecuted for their faith – some were in prison and some were being ill-treated. There might not be any Christians suffering in that way in our church, but we can go wider than that and think of this principle of 'remembering' people.

Notice we are told to remember them as if we were fellow prisoners, or as if we were being ill-treated as well. In other words, we are to think about people and be concerned for them, as if we were in their shoes. Think about what it is like for that person in prison – the loneliness, the poor facilities, the lack of food, and so on. Think about what it would be like to be ill-treated – the humiliation and injustice. And of course, this example of love isn't just about empathizing with people, it's about putting ourselves in their shoes so that we *do* something. The readers aren't told exactly what they should do, but 'remembering' these people like this will lead them into concrete action.

So look around at your church or small group and ask yourself what it is like to be:

- that widow whose children have left home;
- those parents with the rather unsettled young children;
- that person whose work is pressured and who is constantly travelling;
- that person who has recently been bereaved;
- that housewife whose husband works such long hours;
- that elderly person whose health is failing;
- that missionary, away from home.

Answering questions like these will lead to a variety of actions: when a young couple had their first child, their small group thought the best way to help was to supply them with meals for the next fortnight; when someone had cancer and had to make regular trips to the hospital for chemotherapy, her small group helped with practical things like doing her washing and shopping. Then there's the missionary who loves rugby, and whose home church sent him a video of all the Six Nations games. Putting ourselves in people's shoes will lead us to keep on loving as we should.

The power of presence

From there we set sail and arrived at Rhegium. The next day the south wind came up, and on the following day we reached Puteoli. There we found some brothers who invited us to spend a week with them. And so we came to Rome. The brothers there had heard that we were coming, and they travelled as far as the Forum of Appius and the Three Taverns to meet us. At the sight of these men Paul thanked God and was encouraged (Acts 28:13–16).

The principle of love is shown wonderfully in Paul's arrival at Rome. On the way he is shown hospitality, but it's what happens as he draws close to the city that I love. The church in Rome has heard that Paul is on his way, so what do they do? They travel out to meet him. Some got to the Forum of Appius which was a forty-three mile trek from Rome; others got only as far as Three Taverns which was thirty-three miles (you can think about why they stopped there!).

Now look at Paul's reaction when he saw these guys: he 'thanked God and was encouraged'. He saw them coming down the hill and his heart was lifted, and he said, 'Thank you God!' Why was that? Their efforts weren't going to get him to Rome any quicker. They didn't have important business to discuss. They hadn't brought him anything. All they were going to do was turn around and go back to Rome with him.

But you instinctively know why he was so encouraged, don't you? It's like someone coming to meet you at the airport even when they're only going to get the train home with you. It shows they care! You are glad to see them because of the enjoyment and encouragement of people's company. It shows the power of our presence with people, even if we are doing nothing practical to help them at all.

I remember when some missionaries were due to arrive home for a break and we were discussing how they would get back from the airport. There were too many of them to fit in one car, and there was a lot of baggage. We wondered if it would be easier for them to get a taxi home. It was an attractive thought, especially as the people picking them up would have to miss their small group meeting that night. The missionaries would have got home in the same time. But just imagine the difference it would make to them seeing friendly faces there as they walked out of arrivals. We sent the two cars.

Think of how your presence can be an encouragement to people in your church – just your presence, not even doing anything to help. Those who are bereaved often say they simply want company. They don't even need a conversation, just someone else in the house. Those who are elderly with no family around – especially if they can't get out much themselves, but even if they can – really appreciate someone just spending some time.

You can show love just by being there. I say 'just'. This is a way of loving that requires no skill or offering of resources. It just requires time. But in our busy lives, that might be more costly to some of us than giving money.

The mark of the Christian

Christians have chosen a variety of ways to mark themselves out as followers of Jesus. In the past, some have had special haircuts, or special clothes. Some used to wear chains round their necks, or crosses. Today some may pin a cross on their lapel or place a fish symbol on their car.

'Love one another,' said Jesus. Love as I have loved you; love each other unconditionally and sacrificially. That is the mark of the Christian. It is only right that we love each other, given the way God has loved us. It is only appropriate that we love each other, given that we are now family together. And it is necessary for us to love each other, to win the world.

Jesus says people will know that we are his disciples, *if* we love one another. This is part of our witness. We saw that when we were thinking about unity in chapter 2 using John 17 as a base. Jesus said that when the world sees our unity they will know that the Father has sent him. The unity between very different people in the church helps convince the world of the truth of Jesus. The same is true of our love. Our love is in fact simply our unity in action. We love because we are one.

Francis Schaeffer said that this love and unity were the 'final apologetic'. That is, the ultimate defence of the truth of the gospel. He wrote this: 'Love – and the unity it attests to – is the mark Christ gave Christians to wear before the world. Only with this mark may the world know that Christians are Christians and that Jesus was sent by the Father.'

I ask you, as the apostle John did, that we love one another (2 John 1:5).

Study 6

1. What connections does John make between God's love for us and our love for other Christians (see 1 John 3:16–18)?
2. What is John's specific concern in 1 John 3:17–18? Why do you think he stresses this?
3. Look through each of the passages below and ask the following questions:

   - In what way do we see Christian love being practised here?
   - How can we learn from this example?
   - What can I do differently to love people more?

   Acts 2:44–47; 4:32–37

   Acts 6:1–7

   Acts 28:11–16

   Hebrews 13:1–3

   Philippians 4:14–19

7 : Follow your leader

1 Timothy 3:1–13; Acts 20:25–38

'I am certainly not one of those who need to be prodded. In fact, if anything, I am the prod.' (Sir Winston Churchill)

In 2002, the BBC ran its 'Greatest Briton' campaign, where the public voted for a variety of famous British figures. Churchill won that vote. He is remembered of course as one of the greatest leaders at a time of national crisis. He was inspirational, courageous and determined. As his words show, he had great personal drive – he didn't need to be prodded himself, but rather he prodded others into action.

Churchill stands as one of many examples of great leadership. But thinking of his leadership raises questions for us about the church. First, who is to lead us? Who is to 'prod' us into action? Secondly, how are they to lead? What techniques should they use?

It seems to me that most of us simply accept the leadership pattern of whatever church we happen to go to. It may be that when we change churches we come across a different pattern or system. We might prefer it, or dislike it in comparison. But we don't often step back and ask, 'What leadership does the Bible tell us about? What leaders are we to have? What are they to do?'

Who is in charge around here?

The single most certain thing you can say about church leadership in the New Testament is that churches were governed by groups of elders. For example, when Paul and Barnabas go on the return leg of their first missionary journey, we are told, 'Paul and Barnabas appointed elders for them in each church' (Acts 14:23). Then when Paul wants to give some parting instructions to the Ephesian church before he sails away, he calls the 'elders' of that church to meet with him (Acts 20:17).

Then in Titus 1:5 we find Paul explaining to Titus why he was left on Crete: it was so that 'you might straighten out what was left unfinished and appoint elders in every town, as I directed you'. The way Paul refers to it indicates that this is what was needed before the work of establishing the churches was finished.

And then in other letters like 1 Peter and James, which are written to a number of churches, reference is made to elders, on the clear assumption that they would be there in each church. In fact, elders are the *only* commonly mentioned group of leaders. That's why I said the most certain thing about church leadership in the New Testament is that churches were governed by groups of elders.

However, in saying this I have now to point out that elders go under different names. 'Elders' is the most common, but we get some others as well; we read about 'overseers' (traditionally translated 'bishops') and 'pastors' or 'shepherds' (they mean the same thing, to 'pastor' is to 'shepherd').

Some people have debated how these three groups – elders, overseers, pastors – fit together. The answer, I think, is very straightforward. When Paul calls the elders of the church in Ephesus (Acts 20), he refers to them as being 'overseers' of the church. And then he says they are to be 'shepherds' (pastors) of the church. In other words, the elders are overseers, who are the pastors. And we see the same thing elsewhere in 1 Peter 5 and in Titus 1.

So there is only one group here, going under different names. My church currently has seven elders of which I am one. But we could call them all pastors. Or we could call them all overseers (if you like, you could call them all bishops – but I'd prefer it if you didn't).

What do you spend your time doing?

As a church pastor this is a question I am asked from time to time – along with the predictable teasing about working only one day a week. It highlights the fact that many people don't know what a church leader does – or should do.

To describe what a pastor does, I think you have to use a number of terms. The first one is that of *protecting*. In Acts 20:28–31 Paul says this to the Ephesian elders:

> Keep watch over yourselves and all the flock of which the
> Holy Spirit has made you overseers. Be shepherds of the
> church of God, which he bought with his own blood. I know
> that after I leave, savage wolves will come in among you and
> will not spare the flock. Even from your own number men
> will arise and distort the truth in order to draw away disciples
> after them. So be on your guard! Remember that for three
> years I never stopped warning each of you night and day
> with tears.

He urges the elders to keep watch, to protect the flock. The reason is clear: savage wolves will come in and try to kill them. In verse 29 Paul explains that he has used the metaphor of savage wolves to refer to people who distort the truth. These are people who bring wrong teaching of some kind. And wrong teaching does Christians terrible harm. It's like being fed food with traces of poison: instead of nourishing you as it should, it weakens and harms you.

Paul is not referring here to differences of opinion on minor matters. Christians do disagree on what the Bible teaches on many subjects but remain united on the central truths of the gospel. But it is when those central truths are distorted that the poison starts. For example, when Paul writes his letter to the Galatians he says they are turning to another gospel which is really no gospel at all (Galatians 1:6–7). This distorted truth will kill them.

And what Paul envisaged has been true not only in the time of the New Testament but also throughout church history. I think of Rob who was visited by the Jehovah's Witnesses. They deny that Jesus was truly God and reject the belief that we are saved only by faith in Jesus' death. But they can be very persuasive. They usually have very well-prepared arguments. And Rob was struggling. He was meeting weekly with someone from the Jehovah's Witnesses and found himself agreeing with them. He wisely went to one of his elders and explained what was happening.

The elder and Rob spent time together looking at how the Jehovah's Witnesses were using the Bible, and examining their arguments. Rob finally came to a position where he was clear in his own mind why the Jehovah's Witnesses were wrong and was able to tell them so.

Now of course, Rob didn't necessarily have to talk to an elder. Lots of people would have been able to help in that way. But that is exactly the sort of work a leader should be doing. It fits especially with the name of overseer. You could almost translate it 'guardian'. An overseer is to watch over people, looking out for any danger coming towards them, and guarding them from it. It also fits with part of the picture of the shepherd because a shepherd would keep a look out for any danger threatening the sheep. As we'll see in a moment, that means that teaching the truth and correcting error is a key part of what leaders are to do.

The second term we could use to describe an aspect of a pastor's role is that of *feeding*. While the image of shepherd or pastor includes a protecting element, it also includes the idea of feeding the flock. Nurturing them and caring for them, seeing them grow strong. We see this idea when Jesus talks to Peter in John 21 and charges him to feed the sheep and to take care of them (the same word as 'pastor').

This feeding comes through teaching. Paul describes how the staple diet of Christians should be good teaching. So in Titus 1:9 Paul says about the leaders: 'He must hold firmly to the trustworthy message as it has been taught, so that he can encourage others by sound doctrine and refute those who oppose it.' This idea of encouraging people by sound doctrine is concerned with good healthy teaching, rather than the poison of false ideas.

Thirdly, the pastor's work involves *leading*. Paul talks of 'the elders who direct the affairs of the church' (1 Timothy 5:17). By that Paul means ruling or leading the church. And this fits with the term 'elder'. To our ears the word 'elder' simply sounds like someone who is old. But its background is in the Jewish synagogue which would have been run by a council of elders. It conveys a sense of leading and governing.

The same word for leading is used back in 1 Timothy 3:4–5: 'He must manage his own family well and see that his children obey him with proper respect. (If anyone does not know how to manage his own family, how can he take care of God's church?)'

The reason church leaders have to be able to manage their family well is because of the similarity to their role in the church. So we should think of this leadership role in very similar terms to the family. It needs that mix of gentleness and firmness, encouragement and discipline, all under-girded by love and care. And if someone can't do that well at home, then they shouldn't try to do it at church.

Now these three things – protecting, feeding and leading – aren't completely separate. They are connected together. The leaders are basically told by God: 'Look after the church, you are responsible for it and its growth, look out for it, govern it and guide it for the good of the people.'

So how *exactly* do you spend your time?

How do leaders protect, feed and lead?

Teaching

As we have seen already, the leader must be able to teach people in order to help them grow and to defend them from error. This is why in 1 Timothy 3:2 we are told, along with lots of character traits, that the leader must be able to teach. A major part of an elder's role is teaching: that is the prime way that the church grows, and is cared for, guided and protected.

We also see the role of teaching in 1 Timothy 5:17: 'The elders who direct the affairs of the church well are worthy of double honour, especially those whose work is preaching and teaching.'

Two things need to be said about this verse. First, it might read as if there are some elders whose role is not preaching and teaching. At first sight it looks like all elders direct or rule, and some teach and preach within that. Now that is one way you can interpret this verse. But that word 'especially' can just mean 'namely'. In which case, Paul is saying this: 'the elders who direct affairs of the church, namely those whose work is preaching and teaching'. That seems the right way to understand it, because elsewhere we find that elders are always involved in a teaching role. In other words, there is no such thing as a non-teaching elder.

And that leads to the second thing to say. When it says 'preaching and teaching', you might think that means all of the leaders of a church have to stand behind a pulpit and do what we call preaching. But that's not the case. The literal meaning is, 'those who labour in word, and in teaching'. Paul probably says 'labour in word' to cover all sorts of things like encouraging, comforting, warning or rebuking. And there's no specification of how that is done or how the teaching is done. It can be done from a pulpit (I do that most Sundays), but it can also be done in a small group, or one-to-one.

Now we have also seen that everyone in the church is to teach to some degree. And so all this stuff about the leaders teaching must not be taken to mean that the leaders have a monopoly on it. What it does mean is that they lead the church by teaching. And so they are responsible for overseeing all the teaching of the church.

By example

The second way elders lead is by *example*. 1 Peter 5:2–3 says: 'Be shepherds of God's flock that is under your care, serving as overseers – not because you must, but because you are willing, as God wants you to be; not greedy for money, but eager to serve; not lording it over those entrusted to you, but being examples to the flock.'

These verses express very neatly one of the ways that leaders look after the flock. They are to be an example to it. This scares me silly! I am supposed to be an example to other people in how to live the Christian life. I have enough struggles living the Christian life myself! No leader I know of thinks of themselves as the great model of Christian living.

But, while they are not super-saints (no-one is), they are to set an example. This is why Paul gives us a list of qualifications for leaders including things like being 'self-controlled', and not being 'given to much wine' (1 Timothy 3:1–7). Those are things every Christian should aim at, but they are a requirement for the leader because he is supposed to be an example.

When I was learning to drive, my mum took me out to get some practice. But sometimes when she was driving me around I noticed she didn't always do what she had told me to do – she wasn't obeying her own instructions! Being the pleasant teenager I was, I took great relish in pointing this out to her. Mum replied,

'Don't do as I do, do as I say!' That was OK in teaching someone to drive, but it's not OK in teaching people to live the Christian life. Leaders are to teach it and model it. They will constantly fall short themselves – at which point they will model things like confessing and repenting, apologizing and forgiving. And, as with teaching, it's not that the leaders will be the only good models in a congregation – they will probably point at some other great models themselves – but they must be models.

Lead the family as family

In this way, the leaders are to lead the church – God's family. They are to lead it into being all that it is supposed to be. And that means leading it in the sort of family life we've looked at in this book already. In an earlier chapter we looked at some of the unfortunate effects of individualism. Another effect is this: we think of leadership as directed towards individuals. In other words, the leaders of the church should do all this protecting, feeding and leading for the sake of individuals' growth as Christians. They should teach and set an example so that individuals can grow in their Christian life.

Well of course that's part of it. But they should also lead the church into living as a family. They should teach the church about what it means to love each other and serve each other, to use our gifts and depend on each other. And they should set an example in all this themselves.

Think about bringing up children. My wife and I spend time with our kids individually and talk to them about how they are doing, their struggles and hopes, their joys and fears. But we also spend time as a family. And in being parents we have to teach our children how to live with each other: to share toys; to be kind to each other; to say sorry; to forgive each other, and so on. And in doing that, we must be examples of exactly those things.

Well, it's the same in the church. Leaders are concerned for individuals and their growth in their own relationship with God. And to that end their teaching will address personal issues, and they will also spend time with people individually. But they must also be concerned for how the family is living as family. They must teach on that, and must lead the church into living like that.

Paul gives an example of this in his letter to the Philippians. There was a problem there between two women who had fallen out. We don't know the details of their dispute but we do know what Paul said to them, and to one of the leaders: 'I plead with Euodia and I plead with Syntyche to agree with each other in the Lord. Yes, and I ask you, loyal yokefellow, help these women who have contended at my side in the cause of the gospel' (Philippians 4:2–3).

Paul pleads with these women to agree with each other, but he also asks the 'loyal yokefellow' to help. That's a reference to one of the leaders. So Paul expected a leader to get involved in this dispute to help these women live together as family.

I hinted at this idea in an earlier chapter when I described how leaders are like managers of sports teams. Their job is not just to get each individual playing well and growing in his or her ability, but to get the team playing well *as a team*. That involves the relationships between players, their attitudes to each other and their working with each other, not just their 'individual game'.

In fact, we can take the analogy a step further: in some sports you get a player-manager. Someone in this role plays as part of the team and also manages the whole team. That's what church leaders are like. They don't sit on sidelines shouting instructions, they are on the field themselves. And because they are on the field they not only lead with what they say, but what they do. If they don't follow the tactics they tell the team themselves, then no-one else will!

Lead as a team

The last thing to say about elders is to do with how many there should be. When we see leaders mentioned in the Bible they always occur in numbers greater than one. There are no references to *the* elder of a church, but rather the expectation is that leadership is always invested in a team.

Now leading as a team brings all sorts of difficulties. They have to lead together even though they may have differences of opinion; they have to work together even though they may have very different personalities. But that is what we see in the New Testament, and I think God planned it like this for two reasons.

First, it is dangerous to invest total leadership in one person. They can do great things, but there are no checks or balances. Secondly, it misses out on the richness that a team can bring. In a team you get the complementing of each other's gifts and a variety of different perspectives on an issue. I can think of many leaders' meetings when my view on a topic was turned around by the contribution of others in the team. In addition, being a team means the leaders begin to set an example of being 'church' in their relationships with each other. Their own dependence on each other, encouraging each other, forgiving and bearing with each other, will set the tone for the whole congregation.

So team leadership will always be harder work, but we will have better led churches for it.

What about deacons?

By now you may be saying to yourself, 'He's left out one group of leaders; what about deacons?' We know far less about the role of 'deacons' as they are only mentioned a few times in the New Testament. I'm going to say comparatively little about them – but that's for reasons that I hope will become clear.

The name deacon simply means *servant*. But it's clear that this is an actual position in the church because Paul talks in 1 Timothy 3 of overseers and then deacons, and in Philippians 1:1 Paul writes to 'the saints in Christ Jesus at Philippi, together with the overseers and deacons'. So they are not just anyone who serves – after all, we all serve in the church. They are officially recognized servants, servants with a capital 'S', if you like, who have been given specific responsibility to serve in some area.

When we come to their *role*, you will have to forgive me for being obvious here – they serve. We are not told any more than that. There is no mention of them requiring particular skills like being able teach (not that deacons can't teach of course, it's simply that it's not a necessary skill for that role). But they are to be exemplary in their character for the same reason as the elders: to be an example, and they are to carry out their role in the right way. In other words, *how* they serve is very important. And they must be able to manage their households well (1 Timothy 3:12), which must mean that they are to display that loving leadership within the family we talked about earlier.

Many people have turned to Acts 6 for help in understanding the role of deacons. In that chapter we find the apostles arranging for seven men to be chosen who would take responsibility for the distribution of food among the church. The apostles give this responsibility over to these men to free themselves up so they can devote their time to the ministry of the word and prayer. And many have understood this passage as giving an example of the work of deacons. So in many churches the deacons take responsibility for practical areas such as finance, buildings and practical care of the congregation.

These areas of responsibility sum up the general role of deacons well. Leaders should be looking to delegate responsibility like that. Not that they are then no longer interested in it themselves; ultimately they will still guide what happens in these areas and are responsible for it, but they hand over a key role to someone else.

The only thing I don't like about that reading of Acts 6 is it sometimes leads to a 'practical' versus 'spiritual' divide. The elders are responsible for the spiritual stuff and the deacons are responsible for the practical stuff. Actually you can't divide up church life like that – and many practical things have spiritual implications. So in summary, I would say the deacons play a vital role in *assisting* the elders in their work.

So ...

Let me throw out a few things for us to do. First of all, *pray* for your leaders. They face a daunting task, and every leader I know feels inadequate for it. Maybe take some of the verses we have looked at in this chapter and use them to pray for your leaders.

Secondly, *encourage* your leaders. Encourage them to be doing all we have talked about. It is very easy for leaders to get distracted with all sorts of stuff, so encourage them to be focused on the business of leading the church. And don't forget to tell them that you appreciate them.

Thirdly, *respect* your leaders. It is a 'noble task' to be an overseer (1 Timothy 3:1). We British specialize in anti-authority sarcasm. If you listen to any discussion about the government or those in management in a business, you generally hear them being run down, being moaned at and criticized. It's very easy for that same attitude to flow over into the church.

Now leaders might do all sorts of things wrong, and they are never to be beyond questioning or criticism. But it's an ugly attitude that looks only to put them down. Given what we have been looking at and what leaders are trying to do, and given the position God has given them, they deserve the respect of their congregations. So Paul says, 'Now we ask you, brothers, to respect those who work hard among you, who are over you in the Lord and who admonish you. Hold them in the highest regard in love because of their work' (1 Thessalonians 5:12–13).

Finally, give *thanks* for leaders. Give thanks for leaders of the past who have kept your church on track. They might not have done things you would have liked them to do, but they have probably been caring for the church in the way they thought best. And give thanks for your current leaders who are caring as best they can as well.

Study 7
1 Timothy 3:1–13

1. Make a list of church leadership positions from the following passages: Acts 14:21–23; 1 Timothy 3:1–13; Titus 1:1–9; Philippians 1:1; 1 Peter 5:1–4.
2. Are any different names used for the same position (see Acts 20:17, 28)?
3. From the passage in 1 Timothy 3 list the characteristics required for the position of overseer and deacon and briefly define each term.
4. Is there anything striking about these qualifications? How do they compare with the qualities expected of all Christians?
5. What does 1 Timothy 3:1–7 mention about the role of the elder or overseer? (You might also like to look at 1 Timothy 5:17; Titus 1:9; Acts 20:28–31.)
6. What then should we look for in elders? How might this be different from what we are tempted to look for? How should we pray for elders in light of this?
7. The word 'deacon' means servant. What does this suggest about their role?
8. What help does Acts 6:1–7 give us in understanding the role of deacon?
9. Do you need to make changes in your view of church leaders? What difference will that make?

8 : Making it work

Colossians 3:12–17

I know enough about golf to talk you through a really great round. I could tell you how straight my drives off the tee would be and how I would pick exactly the right club to land on the green. I could describe my perfect judgment of the wind and the hardness of the ground, and how my puts would be perfectly judged. I could make it sound wonderful.

But if you put me on the first tee of a golf course, the chances are I would actually make a real hash of it. And if I didn't make a hash of it then, well it would be only a matter of time. The fact is I am rubbish at golf – I could talk a good game, but the reality would be pretty ugly to watch.

Church is like a round of golf. We can describe church life in great detail – how it is all supposed to work, and how wonderful it will be. You might, I hope, have had that feeling reading this book. We have described a great church where very different people are united together, all playing their part in building the body, where all of those commands to love one another and to care and so on are being fulfilled. Where leaders lead well and so on. But then we come to the first tee, where it is time to do it for real rather than describe it, and the chances are we will make a mess of it. And even if we don't make a mess of it then, it will be only a matter of time before we do.

In other words, although church is easy to describe, it's not going to be quite so easy in practice. In fact, as we have talked about it, I hope you have been pushed to think about how great a challenge it is being church together. A German theologian called Dietrich Bonhoeffer put it very well when he said this: 'The sacrifice of time and the setting aside of personal wants/desires and bearing with each other means that community is hard work. As a result many people love the idea of community more than the experience of community.'

'Church' as we have described it sounds great, but it's going to be hard work. It is going to be costly in terms of our time and energy. It will involve setting aside my wants and desires, and putting others first. There will be times when we won't want to live like this because we don't like the personal cost.

And then of course there is a second problem: when we do make the sacrifice to get stuck in, we are going to get it wrong sometimes. For example, we may be encouraged to 'teach one another', and so we contribute in a Bible study. But then we say something that offends someone else in the group. Or we want to 'serve one another', so we offer to help someone practically, but they misunderstand and take it completely the wrong way.

Even when we have the best of intentions, we will get it wrong sometimes – we will be 'clumsy' in the way we use our gifts and how we handle each other. And of course, because we are sinful, we won't always have the best of intentions, we'll be downright selfish sometimes, or proud, or uncaring, or whatever.

When we live together as church it won't be too long before we will say something we wished we hadn't, or we will do something and then wish we had done it differently, or we will not do something and then wish we had, or we will react to something someone says or does to us and then wish we could change the way we responded. Sinful people interacting with each other will lead to problems. And so while church life is easy to describe, it's going to be a bit more messy on the first tee. In fact, the whole round could get pretty ugly.

So what shall we do?

How are we going to respond? We could just be less ambitious. We could simply say, 'Let's not have such high expectations of what church is supposed to be.' It is, after all, so much easier to keep our distance from each other, to avoid being too involved with each other. There will be far less cost to us in terms of time and energy; and there is less likelihood of being misunderstood and offending someone; there is less chance of being let down and hurt ourselves.

So we could go through the motions of church, but keep our distance from each other and lower our expectations of each other. In other words, we could decide not to try to do all we have been reading about. And it's a tempting thought. But I hope you can see that to do so would be to decide not to be a New Testament church. It would be to decide not to be the church Jesus wants us to be.

That is why this chapter is called 'Making it work'. We must think about how we can live like this even when we don't want to because it's too costly. We must think about how we can live like this when it goes wrong, when we are offended or hurt, or when we have offended and hurt someone else. It's going to happen. The only way it won't is if we don't get involved in each other's lives, and that means opting for something that isn't really church at all.

In Colossians 3 Paul is talking about how God's people should live. In verses 12–17 he is talking specifically about how they should live with each other. Why not read them through again given what we have just said about church life?

How do we make it work? There are two things we must do together.

Let the peace of Christ rule among us

Verse 15 is often taken out of context and individualized: 'Let the peace of Christ rule in your heart', we read. In other words, don't be anxious or worried, be at peace. There are verses in the Bible which say that, but this isn't one of them. This verse is not about peace within us, it is about peace between us.

Do you see how Paul points us to the relationship that's established between Christians? He tells us to let the peace of Christ rule because 'as members of one body you were called to peace'. This is what we saw back in Ephesians 2 where Christ had brought peace between the Jew and Gentile. And then we saw it again in 1 Corinthians 12 and Romans 12 where we were united together as a single body. So here as members of one body we have been called to be at peace with each other.

In transplant surgery, the big question after the operation is whether the body will accept the new organ or reject it. Will the body and this new organ work together in harmony, or will there be a fight? Well, that's the idea here: Christ has formed a new body, made up of lots of different parts; in fact, there's not just one new organ, but every bit of this body is new. The possibility of rejection between them is huge. But Jesus has called us to peace. He wants a body where everything works in harmony; where each part co-operates and fulfils its function; where everything works together, where there's no fighting between organs. We're called to peace.

Let the umpire rule

And so Paul says we are to let that peace rule over us. The idea is actually that of an umpire: let the peace of Christ judge things;

let it be the umpire that decides how you live; let it make the decisions.

We are constantly making decisions. In any exchange with someone, any conversation, we make decisions: over how we react, what we say, what attitude to adopt, what to do in response. I know those things come to us almost automatically, but we have control over them, and we decide how to respond. The question is, will we allow the peace of Christ to control our decisions?

Suppose someone offends you. Immediately your anger is raised, and you feel resentment brewing in your heart. Paul says you now have a choice how you will react: you can let anger and resentment win the day, or you can let the peace of Christ rule over it. Let the peace that Christ has brought between you and that person control your reaction.

Just think of a few examples. Someone cuts across you in a Bible study, or ignores what you have said. You summon up the courage to mention a prayer request and then no-one prays for it. You expected offers of help given your illness, but none came. A member of your small group makes a rather sarcastic comment about depression even though they know you struggle with it.

We could go on and on couldn't we? There is no shortage of ways we mess up being church. The big question is, when that happens how are we going to react? Will we decide to let the peace of Christ rule?

That means letting the peace rule in how we react. But sometimes letting it rule is about being proactive. This peace is more than just the absence of hostility – this is the body working in harmony. So we can break down the peace of Christ simply by ignoring one another, just as much as by reacting badly. Sometimes then, that peace needs to control us to make us do something when we are tempted not to.

Just think of a few examples. Phoning someone to ask how they are, even though we didn't want to talk to anyone at the time. Caring for someone when we would prefer to ignore the situation.

Making the effort to be with people, to be at your small group for example, so that we can encourage each other, even when we would prefer a quiet night in front of the TV.

Or what about when we realize that we have been uncaring or have offended someone – what decision will we make then? We could say to ourselves, 'Well I was busy, I didn't have time to help, they'll understand', or 'I'd had a stressful day, so it's not surprising I was bit short with them, they'll know that.'

Well, they might know and they might understand, but wouldn't it help the peace of Christ to rule if we were to say to them: 'I was thinking about yesterday, and I should have helped more, I'm sorry.' Or, 'I'm sorry I sounded harsh, I'd had a stressful day, but I shouldn't have said that.'

Paul would have us all ask ourselves, in all daily decisions do we let the peace of Christ rule? Will this attitude, this action or this word promote the peace of Christ among us, or will it work against it? Will it live up to our calling as members of one body, or will it fall short of it?

Heart attitudes

Paul also speaks about the attitudes to each other we will need if this peace is going to rule. Let's start with attitudes that will prevent this peace ruling. It's not hard to think of a few is it? Indifference: where we have no concern for each other, where we are not bothered about other people's needs and situations. Pride: where we are obsessed with ourselves, and wrapped up with our own importance. Resentment: where we are consumed by our hurts, and hold on to grievances.

If we have those as the attitudes of our heart – indifference, pride, resentment – the body will pretty soon be tearing itself apart rather than living in peace. Rather than those attitudes which, let's face it, we will all be tempted to have at times, Paul tells us some other attitudes to put on instead. They are listed in verses 12 and 13. Rather than indifference, put on compassion and kindness: be concerned for people, look to see how you can help and care for them, no matter what the cost. Rather than pride, put on humility and gentleness: place other people and their needs above yourself, don't think too much of yourself, be gentle with each other. Instead of resentment, put on patience, forbearance and forgiveness: endure the wrongs done to you, bear with them, be patient with those people who annoy you, bear with those people who hurt you, and don't hold on to your hurt but let it go, forgive them.

If you wanted to sum it up in one word, what would it be? Well, Paul tells us in verse 14: 'And over all these virtues put on *love*, which binds them all together in perfect unity.'

We can mistakenly understand this verse to mean that 'love' binds these other attitudes together in perfect unity. But literally it is 'put on love which is the perfect bond'. I think Paul means that love is the perfect bond between us; it binds us together perfectly. If you know how Paul describes love in 1 Corinthians 13, you'll know why it is the perfect bond: we are to put on love which is patient and kind, doesn't envy, and isn't proud. Put on love which isn't self-seeking or easily angered, and which keeps no record of wrongs. If we put on love like that, we will have the right attitude for letting Christ's peace rule among us.

Dressing ourselves up in love will be hard work though. It will mean being proactive in showing compassion and kindness, in carrying people's burdens, in looking to welcome people and encourage them. It will also mean loving reactively, when we have to bear with someone, or be patient when someone is provoking or annoying. This will mean simple things like thinking the best of people when they do something that offends us, rather than assuming the worst.

And even when people are in the wrong, and they have hurt us, this means having the love that wants to forgive them, the love that keeps no record of wrongs. That is probably the hardest part of this love. Forgiving people can sometimes be a long process because feelings of anger can keep on surfacing, and we have to decide to forgive again and again and again. But Paul says 'Let the peace of Christ rule', put on love.

These are very challenging verses aren't they? You might be feeling a bit daunted on thinking through what they mean in practice. If you are feeling daunted, there are two things to note. First, be encouraged, because this is probably happening already. I have visited many churches and I have always seen people loving each other. Sometimes it has been pretty clumsy, sometimes there have been some blind spots, sometimes it was showed in rather odd ways, but still they were loving each other. So although I don't know your church situation, I would expect this is already happening, at least to some degree. You are probably already doing this yourself – so be encouraged to do it more and more.

But the second thing to note if you are feeling daunted is that's a good sign! I want people to feel daunted, because if we don't feel daunted we haven't really grasped the enormity of the task. And even if we are doing it well already, we can always be doing it better and better. We can never read these verses and say to ourselves, 'I've met all those commands.' So be challenged by these verses. I am.

But Paul doesn't just leave us with that challenge, he also talks about how we will find it within ourselves to let that peace rule, to show that love. And that brings us to one last question: where do we find the inner motivation and resources to show compassion and kindness, to bear with people and forgive? Paul tells us.

Let the word of Christ dwell among us

'Let the word of Christ dwell in you richly as you teach and admonish one another with all wisdom, and as you sing psalms, hymns and spiritual songs with gratitude in your hearts to God' (Colossians 3:16).

When Paul refers to 'the word of Christ' he is talking about the gospel, the message of Christ and the good news of what he has done. He has already referred to that back in Colossians 1:5 where he calls it 'the word of truth, the gospel'. He mentioned it later in that chapter in verse 25, where he calls it 'the word of God' which he was proclaiming to the nations. Now he calls it the word of Christ because I think he wants to link it with the peace of Christ.

So we are to let that word, that message about Jesus, dwell in us. This has the sense of letting it live among us or inhabit us. And we are to let it do that richly or in all its fullness. This verse is often used to encourage people in Bible study, or in memorizing Scripture. That's fine, but why does Paul bring it up here? What has it got to do with the topic? He has been talking about our attitude to each other, how we should love each other and have peace between us; so has he moved on to the topic of Bible study?

Back to the foundation

Well, no! I think Paul is on the same topic; he's simply going back to the foundations between us. The word of Christ is the foundation for the peace of Christ. The message of the cross is the basis of the peace between us. It is through the gospel that we are reconciled to God, and to each other. The message of the cross is what has brought peace in the first place. That's what we learnt way back in chapter 2. And that foundation is where we will now find the motivation and the resources to let that peace rule.

Let me give you an example. Think about forgiveness. Peter asked Jesus a question in Matthew 18:21: 'How many times shall I forgive my brother when he sins against me? Up to seven times?' Peter thought he was being generous forgiving someone that much. What was Jesus' reply? 'Not seven times, but seventy-seven times.' In other words, 'Don't put a number on it Peter, just keep on forgiving.' And then, knowing how hard it is to do that, and knowing how Peter and everyone else would struggle with that,

Jesus told the parable of the unmerciful servant. That servant owed a huge debt to his master – 10,000 talents. That is equivalent to millions of pounds, so of course there was no way he could pay it back. But his master has pity on him, forgives him, and lets him off completely; he doesn't have to pay back a penny. And yet that servant won't himself forgive his fellow servant who owes him 100 denarii, or a few pounds. He has been forgiven an infinite amount but he won't forgive this paltry sum.

That's a picture of the person who has been forgiven an infinite amount by God, but who still holds grudges against his neighbour and won't forgive them. Then the master in the parable says to that servant 'Because I had mercy on you and forgave you your debt, shouldn't you have had mercy on your fellow servant?' He's saying, 'You should have been overwhelmed with gratitude for the mercy shown to you, and so shown mercy to him freely.'

The message of the parable is that if you understand the cross, if you understand what God has forgiven you, you will be able to do it, you will find the resources to forgive others. In fact, it should be the case that if you understand the cross, you will find it hard not to forgive others. And so you see the word of Christ – the good news of the gospel – is the foundation for the peace of Christ. That's why Paul mentions God's example in these verses from Colossians. Back in verse 13 he said 'Forgive as the Lord forgave you.' And in verse 12, he said we are to show compassion and kindness 'as chosen people, holy and dearly loved'. If we really understand how God has treated us, his generosity and goodness, it will lead us to treat others in the same way. The good news of the gospel will lead us to love, forgive and care.

So when we are finding it hard to love someone, or to show compassion and kindness to them, what should we do? Paul would take us back to reflect on the compassion and kindness God has shown us in Jesus. Let God's love in the gospel dwell in you richly.

When we find it hard to bear with each other, or hard to forgive each other, Paul tells us to reflect on how God bears with us, how he has forgiven us. He would take us back to the cross and tells us to reflect on that. Let that word of Christ dwell in you richly, let it exercise its power in your life. As it dwells in you, and you focus on it, you will find the inner resources to live the life of love and peace he has called us to.

That is why there is such a focus on thanksgiving in these verses. Did you notice that in verses 15, 16 and 17 there are references to being thankful or grateful? When you are thankful to God for all he has done for you, it is almost impossible to start bearing grudges at the same time. When your heart is full of gratitude, the most natural thing to do is to show compassion yourself, to be kind, humble and gentle. We need to let the gospel dwell in us richly to produce its fruit of thanksgiving so that we can live like this.

So what do we do?

That sounds great in theory, but how do we let the word of Christ dwell in us richly? Verse 16 tells us: 'Let the word of Christ dwell in you richly as you teach and admonish one another with all wisdom, and as you sing psalms, hymns and spiritual songs with gratitude in your hearts to God.'

That verse might seem to suggest that we are to let the word dwell in us as we get on with the activities of teaching and singing. But the meaning is actually that we let the word dwell in us by these activities. They are how it dwells among us. In other words, we are to be teaching each other the gospel, to be correcting each other about the gospel with all wisdom, to be singing about the gospel with gratitude and so letting it dwell richly among us.

When we come to church on a Sunday, or to our small group meeting during the week, we should come saying to ourselves, 'I hope I will be reminded of the gospel in this meeting. I hope I will be taught about it and corrected in my understanding of it. I hope we will sing about it.' We should hope that the word of Christ will dwell richly among us as we meet. We need to have that happen, because we need to keep on coming back to the cross, and let the wonderful message seep deep into our hearts. That has to happen for us to live a life of love and forgiveness and peace. If we are finding it hard to let Christ's peace rule among us, we need to let Christ's word dwell a little more richly among us.

Study 8
Colossians 3:12–17

1. Go through the list of characteristics that we are to clothe ourselves with from verses 12–13 and put each one into your own words.
2. In what way is verse 14 a summary of all these?
3. Which of these characteristics is most alien to our culture today? Which one do we have most trouble seeing realized in the church?
4. What does Paul mean when he says, 'Let the peace of Christ rule in your hearts' (verse 15)? How does the reason he gives help us understand this command?
5. When are we most tempted not to let the peace of Christ rule?
6. What is being commanded in verse 16? (Hint: look at Colossians 1:5.)
7. In the second part of verse 16, how does Paul say we are to let the word of Christ 'dwell richly'?
8. How does this command to let the word dwell in us help us let the peace of Christ rule?
9. What is the greatest challenge/encouragement to us from this passage?
10. In what ways is the message from here more important than previous material on what we do in the church?

9 : Painting a picture

Acts 2:42–47

Well, we have spent eight chapters thinking about 'church'. On the way I have tried to give some pointers as to what this could look like in practice, but in this last chapter I would like to draw some of the threads together and paint a picture of church life.

To help us in that we are going to look at a passage in Acts 2:42–47. This is where Luke paints a picture of a community of God's people. In fact it's a brand new community because it comes just after the startling events of Pentecost when the Holy Spirit came to live in God's people. That prompted the apostle Peter to give a speech telling people the good news about Jesus, which concluded in verse 38 with a call for people to repent and be baptized. If they do, then they too will be forgiven and they too will receive the gift of the Holy Spirit, he told them. And we are told in verse 41 that 'about three thousand were added to their number that day'.

So it is a brand new church. A new community of God's people. Luke paints his picture of what that community's life looked like. The way he does it is to list their top priorities, the things they devoted themselves to (see verse 42). That word 'devoted' is strong, emphasizing that this is what they gave themselves to wholeheartedly, this is what occupied their time and their energy, this is what they wanted to focus on as a church. In the following verses Luke goes on to describe what that looked like (and the following couple of chapters expand it for us). We need to look at these top priorities and think about what they could look like today.

Devoted to learning

Verse 42 says, 'they devoted themselves to the apostles' teaching'. The Holy Spirit opened a new school that day in Jerusalem because anyone who becomes a Christian embarks on a new educational process. God wants his people to be continual learners.

What do we learn about? We learn more about what God has done for us in Jesus, more about what he is doing now and will do in the future. We grow to know God himself better and so learn to trust him, and live in relationship with him. We learn how that should shape our lives together, what difference that needs to make to my family, my relationships, my work, or my leisure. We devote ourselves to learning.

Notice that we learn from an *authoritative message*. They learnt from the 'apostles' teaching'. The apostles were the ones inspired by God to teach his truth, they were the authoritative witnesses, entrusted with God's revelation. That is why their sermons went into the Bible, and our sermons should come out of it.

So it's not that others could not teach – there would be many teachers in the early church – but all other teachers were to be judged according to how faithful they were to the apostles' teaching. And in all our teaching today we do the same by devoting ourselves to the apostles' teaching as it is given to us in Scripture. All teachers today are to be judged by their faithfulness to that same message.

Learning, not just teaching

Within the church there must be teaching from the Bible, so why haven't I called this section 'Devoted to teaching'? Because they didn't devote themselves to the practice of teaching, they devoted themselves to the apostles' teaching. There's a difference there! They didn't just want 'teaching' to be happening in that church, they wanted to be learning and growing in their understanding.

Now that might seem obvious, but I am not so sure we work it out in practice. Lots of churches are known as places of good teaching – the church where I work at the moment has just such a reputation. I'd far prefer it, though, for a church to be known as a place of good learning! Because that's what the teaching is supposed to achieve.

If we focus on the 'teaching' then we can easily think that if we have decent sermons on a Sunday morning and meaty Bible studies in our small groups then we are fulfilling this priority. Well, we may be, but not necessarily. We have to ask, 'Is all of that teaching, all that input, achieving learning?' If it is not, then we need to make some changes. That may be a change in how we give our sermons, or the way we lead our Bible studies, or how we listen to a sermon or take part in our Bible studies.

So what do we do?

I have mentioned sermons and small group Bible studies because they sum up most people's experience of 'teaching' in their church. But we needn't restrict ourselves to these methods of teaching. Some people think there is something sacrosanct about having a thirty minute monologue from a pulpit, but I can't find that particular mode of teaching actually commanded in the New Testament.

What is commanded is that there must be 'teaching' and so 'learning' going on in each church. That is central to our growth as Christians. It's also clear that the leaders of the church must play a central role in that teaching, as we saw in an earlier chapter. That doesn't mean they do it all but they do oversee it all, and presumably do a large share of it. It is also clear that we must teach one another, so we must create opportunities for everyone to share their insights and understanding with others, as well as those specifically gifted in teaching.

Now how we put that mix together is up to us. Having the leaders of the church preach sermons on a Sunday, and then meeting in smaller groups during the week to teach one another is one way to do it. And it's a very good way. But it's not the only way. We could have a sermon followed by questions and small group discussion within a Sunday meeting. We could have a 'seminar' style presentation rather than a straight monologue. A passage like 1 Corinthians 14 certainly gives us the impression that many people contributed to the teaching when a church gathered, while still being overseen by the church leaders.

Doing things in different ways may help our 'learning' rather better than the ways we currently do things. But this brings us back to the priority – what we want to devote ourselves to is learning from God as he speaks through his word. It's up to us to find the best ways of doing this.

Devoted to 'togetherness'

Verse 42 says they 'devoted themselves to . . . the fellowship'. Now that word 'fellowship' has become one of those jargon words that I'm not sure we understand anymore. For some people it's like a mystical air that descends on Christians as they drink coffee together – often referred to as a 'time of fellowship'.

The word simply means 'sharing'. And people are bound together because of what they share. So we might all enjoy rugby, and that would result in a kind of 'fellowship' between us. But as we have been discovering, Christians share something far more profound than a common interest. We have seen that what we share is our new life in Christ and that results in our being bound together as a new family, or as one body. So to devote yourself to the fellowship is to devote yourself to your new shared life with the rest of your church. That's why I have used the rather clumsy heading 'togetherness' – there isn't a better word in English that captures it.

Devoting yourself like that means having a whole new mind-set. It's deciding to view your relationship with the rest of the people in your church as one of unity and being bound together as brothers and sisters. And that, of course, results in a way of living. For example, they cared for each other by sharing their possessions (Acts 2:45). We looked at that practical care in an earlier chapter, so I will resist the temptation to repeat myself. Instead let's consider this new way of life: 'Every day they continued to meet together in the temple courts. They broke bread in their homes and ate together with glad and sincere hearts ...' (verse 46).

Your worst nightmare?

How do you like the idea of daily church? Does it sound good to you, or is it your worst nightmare? This group had daily church: 'every day they met together'. Now we must remember the context: this was still festival time and they were effectively on holiday. So it's unlikely that daily meetings carried on. But what we must not miss is the force of the fact that a group who basically didn't know each other began spending time together. They began a new life as a community.

If that sounds like your worst nightmare, it's probably because you think of having a daily church service – like on Sundays. But that's not necessarily what's being pictured here. This is a picture primarily of close relationships rather than formal meetings. To use our heading, they devoted themselves to 'togetherness'. They regarded themselves as a community and so they got together.

They did that as a large group in temple courts but also in each other's homes. The picture here is one of shared lives. By contrast we so often share only Sunday services. I want a church where people are in and out of each other's homes, where people relax together, go on trips together, hang out together, and don't *just* sit in the same building on a Sunday morning.

The problem is that we think of the formal part of a Sunday morning service as 'church', not chatting over coffee afterwards, or staying for lunch together, or going to the park together. We have managed to shrink our view of church into an hour and a half of singing, praying and studying the Bible (which, let me repeat, I believe in fervently). But if we are to be church, we must commit ourselves to relationships with each other – our shared life.

Our buildings give us away here – very few of them actually have space for us to mingle with each other. Instead they are designed as places where we can sit facing forwards in rows. Hence we come to benefit from all that happens in the service, but then we leave and have little interaction with each other. In my experience, this is most often found in churches that focus on 'teaching' as the number one priority. As a result, some churches become more like a preaching centre than a family gathering. Please don't think I'm knocking the key role of teaching in the life of the church or have a low view of preaching – I preach myself virtually every week! And as we have just seen, a church that doesn't commit itself to solid teaching will be a very weak place. But the church is so much more than just a place of teaching from the front.

Any suggestions?

What might we do? Well, once again this stresses the importance of smaller groups in the life of the church. If you are rather busy one week, you might say to yourself, 'I'll have to miss the home group this week'; well, that's OK. But you would probably say, 'I won't miss church on Sunday even if I am busy.' This attitude shows that we think a Sunday service is 'church' but a gathering of Christians in a house isn't. We have given way to thinking that church is more about the trappings than the relationships. So when I say this stresses the importance of small groups, I mean it *really* stresses the importance of small groups. Missing your home group *is* missing church, just like missing a Sunday meeting is missing church.

This may also mean we need to change what we do on Sundays, for example, we could have lunch together. It may mean we need to encourage and stimulate more activities where we spend time together. For example, I belonged to one church where the men rarely saw each other outside of Sunday services. As a result, the quality of relationships was poor. We started a men's breakfast where the time wasn't dominated by a talk or prayer, but gave plenty of space to chat. We needed that opportunity for relationships to start to grow.

God forbid that churches become exclusive social clubs! What we need to see is people devoted to the 'togetherness' of the church and showing that in their daily lives. That means spending time together, but not just to enjoy each other's company. Through the men's breakfast we wanted the growth in relationships to result in men praying together, being honest about their struggles as Christians, encouraging each other as husbands and fathers, teaching one another and so on. None of this was happening in the way they related within a Sunday meeting. I can't say specifically what would help in your church, but we need to be devoted to our 'togetherness'.

Devoted to praise

Verse 42 says, 'They devoted themselves to ... the breaking of bread'. That little phrase has resulted in a great deal of discussion because it can be understood in two ways. It may be a reference to the Lord's Supper, or Holy Communion, where they broke bread and drank wine to remember Jesus' death to save them. In which case, it is an act of remembering and praising God for salvation in Jesus. Alternatively, it could refer simply to eating a meal together. We find the same phrase in verse 46, and in that context it probably refers to shared meals in their homes. In which case, it's part of the 'fellowship' we have just been thinking about.

So how should we understand it? Well, given that Luke's list of priorities for this new church has already mentioned 'fellowship', I think it's more likely that the next in the list, this 'breaking of bread', must refer to something rather more than shared meals. But it's also worth noting that I don't think they would have drawn the distinction we do between the Lord's Supper and an ordinary meal. Any time the church got together and had a meal was a time to remember their salvation. It didn't need the formality of a 'church service'. So I think this third priority tells us that they were constantly remembering Jesus' death for them, celebrating it, thanking God for it and expressing their unity together.

But we are also told more generally in verses 46–47 that they gave themselves to praise and thanksgiving: 'they ate together with glad and sincere hearts, praising God'. If someone from outside was asked to describe this community, I think they would say they were a thankful people, a rejoicing people, a people who praised God for all that he had done for them. Central to that would have been their reflection on Jesus and his death for them.

We saw in the last chapter why that is so important. A church must constantly come back to the gospel and praise God for all he has done, and all he will do. That is the heartbeat of who we are in relation to him and in relation to each other. We all have a tendency to 'leak the gospel'. We know it, but it gradually seeps out of us. I know I need to be reminded of it and led into praising God for it. Without that, our Christian life and church life will eventually run dry.

Praising in song

Praising God is more of a general attitude than an activity – it flows from a heart that is thankful for God's grace and mercy. But we do know from later letters in the New Testament that the early churches sang songs together as part of their praise of God.

Wouldn't you like to know what that involved? What sort of songs did they sing, for how long, did people lift their hands in the air, what instruments did they play? We know nothing of the practicalities, but we do know they were a group characterized by praise and they will have expressed that at least in part by singing together.

This is the moment to say something about praising God in song today. This is often described as having a time of 'worship', but 'worship' is not the most helpful word because the New Testament reserves that word for what we do with our whole life. It doesn't so much matter what you call it, as what you think you are doing in it. This can get a bit involved and would take another book to look at properly. But let me make a few points.

We need to make sure we understand the difference between the Old Testament and the New Testament patterns of 'worship'. There are some great similarities between them, but also some profound differences. The differences focus on what happened at the temple in the Old Testament. The temple symbolized God's presence with his people; the 'Holy of Holies' in the centre of the temple was where God 'was'. So as you went further into the temple you got closer to God, except that if you were an ordinary Israelite you weren't allowed to get very close, that was left to the priests. The priests stood between the people and God; they represented the people to God and God to the people.

Sometimes we forget how all that has changed with Jesus. We saw earlier in the book that 'God's house' is now no longer a special building, but God's people, the church. So we must never think of coming to 'worship God in his house'. We must never think of the front of the church building as a more 'holy' place. We must never think that we need someone else to 'lead us into God's presence'. (That's not to deny the helpful way people can lead us in our praise and reflections, but they are never taking us into God's presence – we do that through Jesus [see Hebrews 10:19–22]). We must never think we get closer to God through the help of music, or candles, or pictures or dance.

But unfortunately that's exactly the sort of language many people use, and the ideas that many people have. If you read the cover of a worship CD you will probably find mention of being taken into God's presence – by the CD! Now I really enjoy and benefit from listening to those CDs, but we are retreating to the Old Testament model if we believe that is what is happening.

So what is happening? We need to recognize that we are actually doing many different things when we sing together. In fact, if we take a moment to reflect on the words of the songs we sing we will soon discover that. Some of them are actually songs to each other rather than to God. In these we are reminding each other of the truth of what God has done and encouraging each other to live for him. Other songs are prayers to God – we ask God for forgiveness or strengthening or whatever. These are just another way of praying.

Other songs are statements of what we believe about Jesus' death, or our experience of God now, or the character of God, or what God will do. And as we sing them, we are reminding ourselves of what we believe and are expressing our confidence in it. Still other songs are statements from us to God – statements of love and devotion, or promises of commitment and willingness to serve. Finally, many are songs of 'praise' where we thank God for what he has done and express our joy and our gladness.

It was this last category that kicked off this whole section, so we had better return to it. This new church was devoted to remembering what Jesus had done for them and praising God for it. As we saw earlier, that's an attitude that goes far beyond singing songs – it's a whole response to God and to what he has done. It's a desire to lift his name up and exalt him. That will certainly mean songs of praise, but it will also mean lives of praise. When people look at our church, I want them to see that we don't just have meetings of praise, but that we are a people of praise. A church that isn't characterized by praise is a church that might know a lot about God, but hasn't really responded to him.

Devoted to prayer

Verse 42 says, 'They devoted themselves to ... prayer.' Again, I should point out that just as we do many different things when we sing together as a church, so do we also when we pray: we thank God, we confess our sins and ask for forgiveness, we adore him and express our commitment to him. But the main type of prayer referred to here in Acts 2 is to prayers of intercession, that is asking God to do things.

We see that sort of prayer throughout the rest of the book of Acts. In chapter 4 we see prayer for boldness in speaking God's word in the face of persecution. In chapter 12 we see prayer in emergency situations like when Peter is in prison. We see prayer for people when they are appointed to a new ministry like the servants in chapter 6, and for Paul and Barnabas when they were being sent out in chapter 13. And there's prayer for people when they leave, as when Paul left the Ephesian elders in chapter 20.

This group of believers that we read of in Acts saw themselves as dependent on God and so they called on him in all they did. Or putting it the other way round, for them not to pray was the same as saying, 'We can manage by ourselves, thank you God.' But they knew how reliant they were, and so they devoted themselves to prayer.

Perhaps you have heard of the massive church growth there has been in Korea. The number of Christians has grown from virtually nothing to about a third of the population. If you ask the people there why the church has seen so much growth, they would say 'Because of prayer.' If you are a bit cynical like me, you will probably respond to that by saying, 'Yes, of course ... but what's the real reason?' We are not happy that it might be that simple – that God is answering a people who are devoted to prayer. (One of the largest churches in Seoul has a prayer meeting at 4.30am every day. That's a church devoted to prayer.)

Charles Spurgeon was a minister who had an amazing ministry in the nineteenth century. When he was first called to be a minister in London, he set one condition before the congregation. 'One thing is due,' he said, 'namely, that in private as well as in public, they, the congregation, must all wrestle in prayer.' Later on, when asked why his ministry was so successful, he simply answered 'Because my people pray for me.' And of course, we shouldn't just pray for our ministers, we should pray for each other and for all aspects of the life of the church.

Not another prayer meeting

All of this leads me to ask why the worst attended meeting of any church is usually the prayer meeting? Is it because we don't get very much out of it ourselves and we go only to things we benefit from? I hope we are not quite so selfish as that. Is it because we don't think prayer really matters or really works? I hope we know our Bible better than that. Is it because those meetings are badly run and boring to be in? That may be so, but I hope our priorities would mean we bear with such things, rather than simply not turning up.

You will have to answer that question for your own church and situation. But what is clear is that we need churches committed to praying. Many churches do need to rethink how they organize their prayer life – let's face it, many prayer meetings are poorly structured affairs. We should think about where the church will pray – is it primarily in our small groups, in our Sunday services, at specific prayer meetings (and if so, when should they be), or all of the above? We need to think how prayer information is circulated so that we have a good supply of 'fuel' for prayer and that our prayers are focused (including printed lists, emails, text messages and websites).

We need to think about how to organize our prayer times imaginatively and creatively. We often need biblical guidance to know how to pray, and one of the best ways is to use prayers of the Bible as a model for our own prayers. But the bottom line is we need to get on with it! The church has to be a place where people get down on their knees and pray. Or, to put it differently, the church must be a family who never forgets who their Father is and so constantly turns to speak to him.

What happened to evangelism?

It might surprise you to note that none of these four priorities mentions evangelism. Now that's partly because the focus is on the church's community life together. But did you notice at the end we are told the 'Lord added to their number daily those who were being saved' (verse 47)? I think there's a strong hint there that it wasn't so much specific evangelistic efforts that brought people into the church, but the attractiveness of this new community's life. People around were drawn to the church by the believers' care for each other, their unity, their desire to learn, their joy in the Lord. And this is something we've looked at already – the link between the community life of the church and its witness.

Let me give you an example of this from my own experience. After our first child arrived, my wife and I were provided with an evening meal each day for almost two weeks. It was organized by the small group we were in. A friend of my wife's who wasn't in the church discovered this one day, and she couldn't believe it. It gave her a glimpse of life inside the church, and she was amazed; she never thought such practical love might be part of church life. As a result she was far more open to listen to the gospel. So don't underestimate the witness of our life as a church.

But of course, 'witness' like that will never actually convert anyone. We are told that God was saving people and he presumably did so in the way described earlier in the chapter – through the gospel being proclaimed and people being told about Jesus. We could start thinking about how the church does that – but that really would take another book.

Paint your own picture
Whenever I've stayed with another family I have discovered that they organize themselves a little differently from my family. If there are young kids, the bedtime routine might not be the same. If there are trips out, they might have a different feel. There are little habits and traditions I have never come across before. But

although different families may do things differently, they are still working out the same idea – how to live as a family.

The same is true of churches. I hope you have seen from this chapter and from the whole book that church is more about who we are and what we are committed to than about particular meetings we attend. It is up to us then to decide how that will look. One church may look very different from another, but will still be 'doing' the same thing. Why not think and pray about painting a picture for your church, and your part in it?

Study 9
Acts 2:42–47

1. What did this new church 'devote' itself to?
2. For each of the areas listed in your answer to question 1 discuss:

   - What does devoting yourself to this area mean in practice?
   - What does this mean you will and won't do in the life of the church?
   - Are there any ways you can do these things better?

3. Think back over the studies in this book and consider: What does being part of the church mean? How would you like to change in your involvement in church life?

Further reading

Robert Banks, *Paul's Idea of Community: The Early House Churches in Their Cultural Setting* (Hendrickson, 1994).

D. A. Carson (ed.), *The Church in the Bible and the World: An International Study* (Paternoster, 1987; Wipf & Stock, 2002).

Mark Dever, *Nine Marks of a Healthy Church* (Crossway, 2000 & 2004).

Liam Goligher, *The Fellowship of the King: The Quest for Community and Purpose* (Authentic Lifestyle, 2003).

Richard Keyes, *Chamelion or Tribe? Recovering Authentic Christian Community* (IVP, 1999).

Melvin Tinker and Nathan Buttery, *Body Beautiful: Recovering the Biblical View of the Church* (Authentic Lifestyle, 2003).

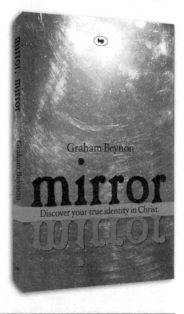

For more details of books published by IVP, visit our website where you will find all the latest information, including:

Book extracts   Downloads
Author interviews   Online bookshop
Reviews   Christian bookshop finder

You can also sign up for our regular email newsletters, which are tailored to your particular interests, and tell others what you think about this book by posting a review.

We publish a wide range of books on various subjects including:

Christian living   Small-group resources
Key reference works   Topical issues
Bible commentary series   Theological studies